TRANSLATOR'S INTRODUCTION

Manuel Devaldès, or Ernest-Edmond Lohy (1875-1956) was a French radical who identified as a libertarian, individualist, Neo-Malthusian, and an anti-militarist. He synthesized these influences smoothly into a practical and humane worldview. The Neo-Malthusians were an English movement which spread to France in the late 19th century; motivated by Thomas Malthus's ideas on the tendency to overpopulation, they advocated for birth control as a remedy for a number of social ills. For Devaldès, birth control was both an essential tool for empowering women and leading to their eventual liberation, and it was a central concept in his militancy against the wars of his country.

He was also part of the broader libertarian or anarchist movement, on its individualistic side; readers of Max Stirner will find familiar terms and concepts here. His important contribution is the marriage of radical individualism with the pursuit of the greater good. His solution was for popular enlightenment by propaganda: as he says, "evolution must precede revolution". When the masses are enlightened they will take measures to strengthen themselves individually, until they are finally able rise against their oppressor, saying: "I refuse to let you steal from me any longer", and will institute "a milieu of free individuals, who are rationally egoistic and committed to one another, and therefore able to make Justice blossom". At once utopian and realistic, it's a worldview of enduring interest.

In this collection of some of his essential essays and pamphlets, Devaldès provides a solid theoretical outline of individualism: a resolutely popular, democratic kind of individualism, as opposed to what he calls its "authoritarian" and "bourgeois" forms. The rest of this collection explores gender differences in individuality, the possibility of libertarian couples and families, libertarian education, and the relations between war and family planning.

POWER, PLEASURE, AND SELF-INTEREST

SUBVERSIVE OBSERVATIONS FROM A LIBERTARIAN INDIVIDUALIST

MANUEL DEVALDES

(1875-1956)

TRANSLATED BY

KIRK WATSON

2016

Contents

REFLECTIONS ON INDIVIDUALISM

1910

Knowledge — Will — Power

I: LIBERTARIAN INDIVIDUALISM AND AUTHORITARIAN INDIVIDUALISM

Few words are more differently interpreted than "individualism". Consequently, few ideas are more poorly than defined than those represented by this term. The most common opinion and the books of popular education take it upon themselves to confirm that individualism is a "system of isolation in human labors and efforts, a system whose opposite is association".

Here we must recognize the common man's understanding of individualism. It is false and, in addition, absurd. Definitely, the individualist is man "alone", and it cannot be thought otherwise. "The strongest man is he who is most alone", as Ibsen says. In other terms, the individualist, the individual who is most conscious of his uniqueness, who has best realized his autonomy, is the strongest man. But he can be "alone" amid the crowd, at the center of society, the group, the association, etc., because he is "alone" from the moral point of view, and this word is here as synonym of unique and autonomous. Thus, the individualist is a unity, instead of being, like the non-individualist, a fragment of unity.

But the uncomprehending, in their coarseness, haven't been able to see the particular meaning of this solitude, its exclusive relation to the individual consciousness, to the thoughts of man; they've has transposed its meaning and, in their dogmatic and absolutist mental habits, have thought only of the economic activity of the individual in the social environment, making him an unsociable being, a hermit, — hence the sham and the absurdity of the definition cited above. Whether we characterize the individualist by saying "he who is alone" with Ibsen, or the "unique one" with Stirner, these Neanderthals will take it literally and will never follow the spirit of our words. Their incapacity to interpret the word correctly causes mistakes, which it's important to reveal, alongside the truth.

If this lowbrow conception of individualism is false, it's not because nowadays people who call themselves individualists live like others in society, for our present societies impose certain associations on the individual: the individual endures such associations, but given that this is not his will his participation ends there. From which we may infer that individualism, consequently, is not the opposite of association: see how a good number of anarcho-communists, who are at last giving "communism" a less religious, less Christian meaning, also call themselves individualists. Max Stirner himself, one of the leading lights of the individualistic philosophy, recommends, in his immortal book, *The Ego and His Own*, the "association of egoists". Finally, the most convincing approach is to look deeper into the question, after which we see that, given the character of individualism, this conception of life doesn't require the physical or economic isolation of individuals in practice, and, consequently, is not against their association.

Most of the opinions and convictions of the "compact majority" are based on definitions of this sort, which, passing to the dignity of clichés, formulate prejudices which are had to uproot, which the pretentious ignorance of certain "intellectuals" and also the interests of certain others who are more enlightened transmit to the humble ignorance of these men of the herd. Despite being an intellectual, one remains no less a man, i.e., subject to natural laws. But it's the natural order for the strong to absorb the weak. Thus, certain intellectuals may appear to be half-savants to the common, self-emancipated people with a passion for the truth. But the latter have managed to learn and surprise, as the savants in question are aware; but they won't say so, since they all have an interest in keeping things as they are, for the perpetuation of their bourgeois privileges; and it only endures because of the half-baked science that's served up to the masses, that is, because of deception, they keep silent or only say part of the truth.

Observe, in present societies, the differences in the education of the proletarians and the privileged. There you have whole secret of the method. A common man, a graduate of primary education, is duly unaware of what individualism really is, and above all what it's based on; it will therefore never inspire him to lead his own life; he's fated to be absorbed by the strong; and this is perfect, — from the State's perspective, or those who could rightly say: "We are the State". On the other hand, a man of the "elite", who received secondary or higher education, has a perfect idea of individualism and its scientific bases. For him it's the very truth, but a truth which he keeps to himself. What an excellent *struggler[1]* he is! He can win: he's armed while others are disarmed. For he'll remember it all the time to further his interests and he will keep the herd wandering astray in the tracks of its precursors. Some truths are better left unsaid...

From the individualism which, by essence, is libertarian, he will fashion a bastard and two-faced

---

[1] (Translator): This is in English in the original.

philosophy (activity at the top, determinism at the bottom of society), justifying all the misdeeds of the ruling class. Hence the relatively precise distinction I've had to make, in order to be understood by a misinformed public, between libertarian individualism and bourgeois or authoritarian individualism. But, ultimately, there is only one individualism, which is essentially libertarian, and fundamentally anarchic.

When libertarian individualism, the true individualism, arms the weak, this is not with the view that they, having become strong, should then oppress other individuals who remain weaker than them, but rather so that they should refuse to be absorbed any longer by the stronger, — the so-called bourgeois or authoritarian individualism only tries to legitimate, by ingenious sophisms and a false interpretation of the natural laws, violent actions and successful cunning.

Lamarck, Malthus, Darwin, and their successors certainly never expected that their discoveries, from which the individualistic philosophy flows directly, could be put to the service of such a Jesuitical work; however, it was inevitable that strength would monopolize right away and would profit by this as by everything else. But all truth bears the seeds of future benefits. The benefits of their works and their consequences is becoming more and more real. In our times, the common people are learning, whether alone or cooperatively; they are becoming familiar with analysis, reasoning, and criticism; they seek to discover their own nature, the motives of human action, the mechanism and forces of the machine that oppresses the weak, the natural laws, and the social realities. The herd is becoming more and more individualized. The individual works at self-realization according to his definition: a unique and autonomous one.

And so he is gradually convinced of these primordial truths:

Power is *knowledge*.

Weakness is *belief*.

II: THE INDIVIDUAL

As understood by the individualistic philosophy, the individual, a potential capacity for uniqueness and autonomy, is not an entity or a metaphysical formulation, but a living reality. It's not like Fichte thought, while critiquing Stirner's "Unique One": a mystical Ego, an abstraction, whose ridiculous and harmful veneration would end in the negation of sociability, which is however an innate quality of man, productive of moral needs which must be satisfied under penalty of suffering.

With this very particular religious character, individualism would be the equivalent of a stupid automatic isolation, like a barbaric and incessant struggle where man would lose all ancestral gains and all possibility of progression. The cult of this abstract Ego would bring slavery, just as from the cult of the Citizen, — The Man[2] of positivism — the modern servitude is born, which is characterized by the associationist and solidarist constraints of

---

[2] Throughout this work, when I capitalize nouns and articles, I mean to express the *holiness* of ideas, according to the spirit of the mystical or the positivist religions.

contemporary society which the State imposes on individuals.

Surely not, the individualistic ego is not an abstraction, a spiritual principle, or an idea: it's the bodily ego with all its attributes: appetites, needs, passions, interests, forces, thoughts, etc. It's not the Ego, — the ideal; it's *me, you, him,* — specific realities. Thus, the individualistic philosophy bends with all individual variations, these having for their motivation the interest which the individual attaches to facts and things, and for a regulator the power at his disposal. By this it establishes a natural harmony which is truer and longer lasting than the artificial and completely superficial harmony of the religions, the dogmatic moralities, the laws, forces of ruse, the armies, the police, the penal colonies and the gallows, forces of violence employed by the authoritarians.

Individualism only moves in the domain of reality. It rejects all metaphysics, all dogma, all religion, and all faith. Its means are observation, analysis, argumentation, and criticism, but the individualist grounds his judgment by a criterion of its own making, and not one he might take from the collective reason which is presently held in honor. Individualism repudiates absolutes, it only cares about what's relative. Finally, it places the individual, the only living and unique reality, capable of autonomy, as the center of every moral, social, or natural system.

— Certainly, my dear professor of morality, our navel is the center of the world, as you say when you accidentally stray into the land of Irony. It is the center of the world for each of us individualists as much as for you, Mr. Slave, or rather Slaver; only we say it aloud, while you carefully hide it while somberly teaching the opposite.

I am for *myself, you* are for *yourself*, and *he* is for *himself* is the center of the world!

Don't laugh. To the degree that God loses, in each of us, this ancient prerogative of being the center of the world, the goal of our actions, the usurping motive of all we do, — as each of us snatches this prerogative for himself. But first, every metaphysical absolute, which are so many divine avatars, must have been joined to God in His nebulous flight of a somewhat grotesque phantom. Our reason then proclaims the permanence of relativity, — and it goes from relativity to ourselves, naturally.

— Where, my Christian contradictor, do you place the center of the world?

— In God.

— And you, Mr. Positivist, Mr. "Atheist", who thinks he no longer believes in God, because you gulp down the anticlerical sausage on "Good" Friday[3]?

---

[3] (Translator): A reference to a republican and anticlerical tradition in certain parts of France, dating back to the mid-

— ...

— A pair of ostensories offer themselves to your believing eyes, and you no longer know which to choose. World-centers, you have plenty, and to spare. In the domain of the sacred, you have an embarrassment of riches; you easily gravitate around this or that center, depending on the situation. And so you're the same wretched creature as your neighbor the theist, if not worse: at least he knows only one God. In the world you operate in, you find the center everywhere but where it really is, and where you ought to notice it: in yourself. Of your own will, — do you actually have only one will? — Of your ignorant will, you're only a satellite turning nonstop around illusory centers, which you think are divine to some extent. Meanwhile the priests of all faiths, both clerical and secular, do their jobs as brigands and robbers.

I, the individualist, am the center of all that surrounds me. Thus, my activity outputs, all that I do, whether by reason or passion, whether premeditated or spontaneous, has a goal which is always my personal satisfaction. When my activity is directed towards another, I am certain that its outcome, whether material or moral, will ultimately come back to me. It's up to other people to do the same.

---

nineteenth century, referred to as "banquets républicains" and "banquets du "vendredi-dit-saint" ("so-called good Friday banquets").

I have a personal morality, and I rebel against Morality; I practice a personal justice and I refuse to worship Justice, and so on.

I'm the sage and you're insane, I'm free and you're a slave, I'm a joyful man and you're a man of grief...

*
**

The primary meaning of individualism is thus summed up in its opposition to entities, to abstractions which are said to be superior to man and in the name of which he is governed, the only reality which exists for him: the individual, man, — not the positivists' Man, "the essence of man", the individual who's been citizen-ized, voter-ized, mechanized, annihilated — the man who *I* am, who *you* are, who *he* is: — *himself.*

Against the interests of the imaginary divinities, I oppose *my* interests. To every supposed Superior Cause, I oppose *my* cause.

In this way, everything in religious philosophy and, consequently, in every religious social system, which emanated from the individual, inferior, vile matter, a despicable atom, a mere unity, to end in these entities, these divinized abstractions and to remain their property, the individual being thus dispossessed, — it all remains the individual's property; the abstractions which have been able to enter the human mentality in order to express inter-individual relations which are, from now on, stripped of their false superiority and sanctity and reduced to their basically utilitarian role; from now on stripped of all their acquired virulence.

And so there will be no more sacrifice of the individual to Society and its priests, to the Fatherland and its priests, to the Law and its priests, and to God or the Gods and their priests. Man finally becomes the sole beneficiary of his labor, he owns everything whose conquest drives his efforts and hard work.

What is society but the product of a gathering of individuals? How can society have any interests (if so, why not appetites, feelings, etc. as well)? And if it could have interests, how could these be superior and contrary to the interests of the individuals who compose it, if they are free? What nonsense or what a hypocritical offense isn't it, then, to create individuals for society instead of creating society for individuals?

Can we, individuals, not replace the State with our free associations?

Can we not replace the general, collective law with our mutual conventions, which can be revoked when they hinder our well-being?

Do we need the divided countries which our masters have made, when we have a bigger one: the Earth?

And it goes on like that. The individualist's free inquiry resolves all these questions fully to the advantage of the individual.

Doubtless, those who make their living by lying, who rule through hypocrisy, the masters and their staff of priests and politicians, may have a different view since their narrow, very narrow interests take them there. But as for me, an individualist and a working man, whose interest is no more in wanting to rob others than to be robbed by them, I cannot think like this and I rebel against it.

And they will avenge this insurrection by discrediting me. So be it. The individualist is abhorred by the masters, the valets, and the sheeplike masses. All of that is eminently understandable. And it will be the norm as long as ignorance is the queen of the world. If the individualistic thinker wants to be treated fairly in his words and deeds, he will have to wait for a distant age of reason — further along the evolutionary tree... But he has nothing to do with the justice of others. His own is good enough for his immediate satisfaction.

When individualism becomes the general rule, the individual will in no way be dispossessed and chained up: he is the owner of the product of his labor and he is independent. As for the parasites who have made their living from this belief in illusory Superior Causes, demanding the holocaust of inferior beings, they will be forced to become producers like everyone else — or to vanish.

*
**

After what I've just shown, that aristocratic thought of Voltaire's, who saw the people — the rabble, to use his term — as a herd to be fleeced, makes so much sense: "If God didn't exist, we'd have to invent him." There must be a God so that the pretext of His mysterious will, His religion, His adoration, may serve to keep the masses of individuals in a state of servitude which will serve the profits and privileges of all kinds of priests, and especially of the masters.

In addition, Bakunin's proud wisecrack now shines brightly: "If God existed, He would have to be abolished!" If God existed, He would imply servitude to a true Superior Cause, He would dispossess man of his due; He must not be allowed to exist, if man's liberty and happiness are to prevail.

Laplace said: "The hypothesis of God is useless". The sciences have progressed since then; the result of their investigations in the domain of man and human societies leads us to say: the lie of a God is harmful, which Proudhon affirms in another way with his famous aphorism: "God is evil." For the cause of God is the Superior Cause *par excellence*, which creates all the other elevated, divinized causes and abstractions, with their apparatus of rights and duties, rewards and punishments, based on the idiocy of free will.

What's the point of killing God if we give birth to *the divine*? As long as man is persuaded of the existence of causes superior to his own, he will inevitably, and, as it were, legitimately, lose his true autonomy; his uniqueness will be only a word: the phantom called God, in His various and coexistent avatars, will steal all his joy.

III: EGOISM AND ALTRUISM

As I've said and as we'll soon see, individualism does not lead to any *a priori* isolation, or any obligatory association: it adopts the regime of liberty. The individualist is neither a hermit nor a herdling; he's a sociable man like anyone else; but he's different on this point: he thinks that his instinct for sociability shouldn't bring him unhappiness and slavery, but should only be a source of joy, prevailing in liberty.

The Nietzschean "teacher", obsessed with "hardness", the "superman", who has long been too gladly seen as a simple individualist: he may indeed be one, but he is certainly also a ferocious beast, against whom men of human character must guard against, if this supposed superman might ever exist in a libertarian world.

Our individualist, on the other hand, is a creature of reason, and if an instinct led him to ferocity, which is unlikely, or at least would be an exceptional case, his reason would quickly teach him that it is in his interest not to be the predator exalted by that simultaneously genial and mad bard, Zarathustra. The predator is not all that different from his prey...

Let's draw out the nuances: he won't perpetrate the deeds of the unleashing of this instinct because they're called "evil" by dogmatic morality, any more than he will do other kinds of things simply because they are labeled as "good", but instead because it will be *in his best interest* to avoid perpetrating the former and doing the latter, for in this way he'll satisfy, in conformity with his naturally calibrated liberty — that is, his capacity, his power — his egoism, which life proclaims to be his primordial interest.

Living is indeed the only goal of life. But *to live* is to be happy. And happiness is not found in a murderous struggle, in primitive savagery. Individuals therefore have an interest in good relationships, concord, and peace, but they are only able to win these goods when they *know how*.

Knowing, — knowing why and how they act, knowing the true motives and the naturally legitimate aims of their actions, this is what will help men avoid the causes of discord and will give a pacified nature to the inevitable struggle for life. In this way, life will gain a sincerity and an ease which is unavailable by practicing the dogmatic moralities.

Individualism contains the realistic view of existence, since this view has philosophical roots in the observation of nature, experimental science, and truths which are acquired and demonstrated, truths whose vital conclusions it pushes to the extreme limits as these are compatible with human reason, with the understanding that this reason — which is our personal reason, not Reason, i.e. some goddess called "Reason" — does not exclude passion, of which it is an auxiliary. At this limit is the relative welfare of man, developing in a liberty regulated by the individual's self-interest.

That's to say that individualism is also a rational, reasonable conception — not rational like the liberals, who are far too "reasonable", but like the libertarians, infinitely less "reasonable"...

*
**

One of these definitively acquired truths is at the root of the individualistic philosophy: that egoism is the only motive of human actions.

Egoism! What a despised word, quite hypocritically despised! What a reviled sentiment, vilified by our professors of morality and by the lemming masses! An old Tartuffe... and yet, egoism guides all our relations with others, and there isn't a single one of those who profess righteous horror on the subject who isn't moved by in the same way, fails to feel it to some extent, or ever ceases to obey it. Even when it seems like a person isn't acting selfishly, he is indulging it completely.

The moralists, naturally, assure us that egoism is a "vice", the "vice of the man who relates everything to himself." What a miserable creature, what an ignoble being is he who pushes vileness to the point of relating everything to himself! He is obviously more agreeable for the master, who relates all things, if not openly to another, or at least to The Idea, The Sacred Idea. Behind The Idea, the "other" is hinted at. In this way nothing is lost... for the ruler, the owner, the priest, the lackey, the whole leadership and everything repugnant in it.

We say that egoism is a virtue, not in the religious sense which dogmatic morality attributes to the word "virtue", but in the scientific sense: it's a force, a vital virtue maintained in man from birth onwards, which is refined and strengthened as his self-awareness expands. The more attenuated it is, the less combative force the man has, the less will to life, the more apt he is for self-sacrifice to the strong, who would subjugate him. The more accentuated it is, the more potential life the man carries, the more will to life he has.

Nietzsche is talking about egoism when, quite rightly, by remaking the table of moral values, he places the "will to power" foremost, and, it's for the preservation of this vital force in man that he condemns the "slave morality" of Christianity. Where he goes wrong is in assimilating power to domination and opposing the slave morality to the "master-morality". Why not simply oppose it with a morality of free men? Then, his idea of existence wouldn't have ended in savagery, in tyranny, in slavery, in a social ideal which, if realized, might be of less value than present conditions.

The reward in the afterlife, dreamed up by theists and spiritualists and promised to the faithful of every religion by its priests, shows that the initiators and continuers of faiths knew human nature well, and that man always acts in his own self-interest.

While making people practice *artificial altruism*, that is, self-sacrifice, during their lives, for their own profit, the priests simultaneously make them work for the illusory satisfaction of an egoism whose interest is closely tied to ultra-terrestrial rewards. This, one will agree, is a supremely wise egoism: why not sacrifice time to eternity...

How ridiculous! But also what well-constructed scam, and notice how nicely that explains the theists and spiritualists' fear of materialism, which will ruin everything. It's a whole industry threatened with ruin, the churches expropriated — without indemnity, a divine bankruptcy. It's true that the priests will only need to switch faiths. From the celestial they can jump to the terrestrial. The divine steps down in favor of the civic. The churches of the social religions hand over their drumsticks to the defectors from the theistic churches. This is what the cleverer among them do, but that path is already so full! You'd have to make God change his skin again. That's easy to say, but not everyone is up to the task...

As soon you notice this identification of egoism with vital energy, this close relationship between egoism and life, you begin see that all those who live parasitically from a necessarily ignorant proletariat have an interest in persuading their slaves of the existence in them, the parasites, of the spirit of sacrifice, of abnegation, of devotion, and ultimately, of altruism, — and then to try and artificially create this altruism in these slaves. For this purpose, they present egoism to man from childhood up as an ignoble feeling, which everyone should get rid of, to reach a supposed state of moral dignity, of purity in feeling, a magnanimity, which is only a state of idiotic weakness. With the theistic priest, one must be a good subject of God's; with the social priest, one must be The Man, The Citizen. It amounts to the same thing: in neither case must one be *oneself*.

But fortunately, even though by this work of enslavement, which is as old as civilization, they often get an all too appreciable result, our moralists have been unable to utterly defeat human nature. I've said that no living being can escape its laws. "Chase out nature; it will come back at a gallop." With each pressing necessity, egoism demands priority over all artificial feelings, thus creating the internal conflicts which disturb modern man, saturated as he is with prejudice and respect, the imprint of religiosity, his being unaccustomed to any natural, free, and passionate desires, and with whom nature is locked in permanent struggle, against the dogmatic and anti-natural morality.

Shall I give a typical example of this reconquest of egoism over the spirit of sacrifice?

The cult of The Fatherland requires a high birth rate, so that the territory situated underneath the invocation of this divinity can be protected against the invasion of those who worship at a different patriotic church. But in France, for example, if we examine the present fact of depopulation, outside of its mostly automatic determinism, that is, if we consider it from the individual angle, as a phenomenon consciously willed by particular individuals, we note that the priests of The Fatherland can implore patriots whose ear they have, both male and female, as much as they want, to make the cannon fodder necessary for the worship of their idol, but these patriots, who have a greater physical and economic interest in not reproducing, they will willingly abstain from doing their "duty", which would immolate this interest on the altar of The Fatherland by creating a numerous family. Over their duty, their fictive religious interest, they rationally prefer their real interests, their personal interests, — but this doesn't excuse them, as they see things, — these puppets, — from jingoistic tirades.

Is it necessary to add that the priests of the Fatherland themselves are the first to avoid having many children? That goes without saying...

*
**

Egoism affirmed is altruism denied.

Altruism is, in a general sense, — since it can take on various forms and different labels in the minds of moralists, — the "virtue" which is opposed to it.

But altruism is a myth. Its greatest value, as far as I'm concerned, is its non-existence. It doesn't exist in man in a natural state, which is, rather, all about egoism.

I can turn over and analyze human actions, but I will never find a single one which is not inspired by egoism, i.e., which doesn't have for its object the contentment of the actor, I cannot imagine an individual who, without being sick or demented, gives himself to another, without securing beforehand the satisfaction of his ego, at least within the limits where the most imperious need of his own preservation imposes on him.

That, given the right circumstances, the act of an individual, while satisfying him personally, should also satisfy the egoism of the person towards whom he directs himself, this is not only possible, but it occurs frequently, and is necessary for the realization of the free association of egoists which we foresee. But there is nothing here which can be called altruism or even disinterestedness, since the individual's only motive is the will to satisfy his passions.

Directly and naturally, I repeat, altruism does not exist. It can only happen indirectly and artificially, through the religious intervention of sacrifice. Thus is it no longer so-called altruism practiced spontaneously: it's *duty*.

Let's take as an example two manifestations of individual activity from which the satisfaction of the other person concerned may result.

When an individual gives himself to another in any way whatsoever, freely, by affective passion, he only gives into a natural need, his own: this is a simple mode of manifestation of egoism finding satisfaction.

But when the individual gives himself to another, under compulsion by the dogmatic morality, by *duty*, in brief, there is a *sacrifice*. Altruism can only exist in this way, coming by surprise and under compulsion. However, do observe that, at the root of the act there is also egoism, since the individual thinks he is satisfying himself and acting in his own best interest by fulfilling his duty.

In the first case, we've had a free act — and not in the second.

Which leads me to say that altruism is artificial and occurs only as a duty, under the influence of a moral constraint, — and that every deed done freely is an egoistic act.

Given that altruism or self-sacrifice is only produced indirectly and artificially, under the constraints of persuasive authority, the power of deception, and by the religion of an alien idea, it follows then that whatever is instead done through passion, freely, driven only by one's own idea, or an idea assimilated to oneself under the emancipatory influence of free scrutiny, — then it is egoistic.

When the individual knows this, he raises his guard against every attempt at theft and murder by the band of "altruists", "philanthropists", and "humanitarians" who take an interest in his lot... to guarantee their own.

It only remains for him, as if by a final necessity, to obtain real power, to elucidate the question of his personal approach and to gain the greatest possible sum of practical knowledge.

In brief:

The egoist — the natural being — satisfies himself by passion. He's the individualist, the irreligious one.

The altruist — an artificial being — sacrifices himself by duty. He's the sacrificial victim, the religious one.

*
**

As the will to sacrifice oneself doesn't exist with man in a natural state, the need to create it originates with those individuals who wanted to live parasitically from the labor of others. This was the endeavor of all the priests, both clerical and secular, of all faiths and religions, whether theistic or social, from the most mystical to the most positivistic.

At the same time they are annihilating the individual in theory, by regarding him as a negligible quantity in their systems, — practically, by education, moralization, they make this annihilation real by fettering the individual to all kinds of abstractions and to the authoritarian institutions placed under their aegis.

They have achieved this tour de force of obscuring man's egoistic feelings and diverting his attention to Ideas, — behind which they lie in wait, they, the priests, and their teachers, these partners in profit. Man's weapons were in his head: ideas. The priests came and externalized ideas; they set them up as if they were real things, superior to man, and populated his "heaven" with them. From then on, man was a machine working for The Ideas, subordinating his real interests to them and only holding in the hollow of his hands the precise quota needed to carry on his slavish tasks.

It's grotesque, it's mad, and yet that's how it is. The most intelligent among these religious mental handicaps have gone so far astray from the natural view of the things that they truly believe they are toiling for their own good, for their own happiness. The priests, surely so; but the faithful, no.

IV: THE LIBERTARIAN MORALITY OF INDIVIDUALISM

Having seen that egoism is the only motivation behind human action, the individualistic philosophy institutes a libertarian morality based on egoism; but, recognizing that the latter is satisfied in various ways according to the individual's level of evolution, it recommends that man work intensively to acquire this science aiming at an ever-increasing and ever more precise knowledge of his *real* interests. To the knowledgeable man, it will quite logically seem that his interests reside far from any religious, altruistic sacrifice, but rather in egoistic satisfaction, in irreligion.

Besides, having observed, not only the natural inequality between men, the existence of the strong and the weak, but also the fact that strength is rendered effective only through the support of the weak who are subjugated by the religious tool of duty, it shines a light on the deception of "laws" and denies the authority of any origin besides force and, consequently, all legitimacy. And so it repudiates all benevolent submission to this authority, whether in agreeing to be the leader or to be led by one.

Never forget, that human egoism, — which will last as long as the species — is the obstacle to the possibility of "good authority" and the existence of "good shepherds". Authority can only be bad, and all shepherds will always be "bad shepherds."

Experience confirms this fact. The Catholic priest comes into power, governing men: he naturally begins by using his authority to satisfy all his needs; for that, he takes from all the producers within the Catholic Church. But observe how the positivist priest supplants him in this government... and he acts in the same way with the workers enrolled in his own church. However, in the gradation of moral values, the so-called advanced minds consider those of positivism to be nobler than those of Catholicism. Neither of these two churches contain any fewer masters and slaves, parasites and proletarians.

The label changes, but man remains.

So long as each individual is deprived of nourishment from the individualistic philosophy, he will be unable to bring his own egoism — a self-aware and well-informed one — in opposition to the invasive egoism: there will necessarily be masters and slaves.

*
**

— If egoism is the obstacle to good authority, would it not be good to try and extirpate it from human nature? The moralist will say, often with sincerity.

The reformer of nature is always amusing to watch... because of his weakness.

— You're a miserable worm, you're ignoble by nature, he says to mankind.

And here is the initial source of the moralized man's misery. I say initial, for God himself originates from this primordial belief. He thinks he's unclean, how sad! He's been told so: and he believes it. If, on the other hand, we can't find a justification for a possible pride in every man, even less will we find one for humility, which is the religious *vice* par excellence.

In brief, the individualistic morality aims at an adaptation of society to nature, directed at the relative happiness of the individual.

What will this individualistic morality be? Oh! It will be quite immoral... From the start, it will not be taught — however, it will be practiced. It will, therefore, be the opposite of dogmatic morality. It will result from scientific instruction and the example of the educative environment. The teaching of morality will be avoided, and people will be content simply to practice freely on its basis.

For example, man will not be told: "Be an egoist", but he'll be told: "Men act naturally according to egoism". There is an abyss between these two phrases, between this order and this observation. And so it's not a case of replacing an old dogma with a new one; man will be taught, and on the basis of what he learns, he will build his *own* morality, *his* unique and autonomous morality, — an individualistic and libertarian morality.

The utter inability to produce a truly beneficent effect, which is common to all moralities heretofore held in honor, has its source in their principle as much as in their development. This principle is contempt for human nature. In this case, contempt is stupid; adapting to the thing would make more sense.

*
**

A general modern fact points to the possible results of an adaptation of morality to human nature and the potential welfare to be gained from it: I mean the anti-militarist, pacifist, and anti-patriotic movement. The tendencies behind it are individualistic, in the sense that they have issued not only from egoism, but from an egoism which is conscious of its *real* interests.

Two goods are especially dear to the healthy man: material liberty (of which the intellectual and moral liberties are consequences) and life. His *real* interests lead him to seek and acquire this material liberty as broadly as possible and to protect his life while waiting for this enlargement. And if there's one thing that constitutes an attack on his liberty, it's militarism, the most frightful maker of enslavement,

35

and if there's another thing that threatens his existence, it's war.

The contempt for militarism, the hatred of war and, consequently, the repudiation of the idea of a fatherland, (simultaneously the cause of and pretext for these social calamities) in the individual's mentality, like the actions which they might cause are, thus, marks of his knowledge of this *real* interest.

A positivist will tell you that this new orientation of conscientious human will is driven by a love of Humanity, — a misunderstood one, he'll add, because if the positivist is a pacifist, the fatherland is still useful to him and the army is still necessary... If this religious man could or would see beyond the outlines of his theology, he would notice that it's not because of any devotion to the idea of humanity that the conscientious individual rises against militarism, war, and patriotism, but rather by the affirmation of a personally and directly self-interested egoism.

However, our positivist might seem to have a point if the individual limited himself to aspiring to his individualistic ideal, but when this individual brings his actions into conformity with his ideas, and abstains from fulfilling what the priest of The Fatherland calls his patriotic duty, what can our positivist then say? Nothing, for his error or his lie is exploded: the individual is acting like this for his own sake and not for others, or for an idea.

When you hear the cry: "War on war!" be certain that the speaker is thinking much less about others and that, in his heart of hearts, he is screaming: "Long live *me*!" If we want to get to the bottom of things, then, we must see that what leads man into theoretical anti-militarism, pacifism, and anti-patriotism, and often to act according to his thoughts, it's the *intelligent and respectable* "cowardice" which makes him cling to life, to his life, since there's only one life.

— This man is a coward, the moralist will say.

Why?

Does the moralist really know why? He only repeats phrases which other asses once recited in his ears.

However, we know that this man is a "coward" because he refuses to sacrifice his life for the defense of his masters' interests, to guard their property. This is where the utility of the dogmatic morality makes itself felt... for the masters.

Well, then! I love this "coward" who wants his freedom of movement and who refuses to absent himself from life's banquet, no matter how poor a figure he cuts at the meal. He's a simple and human hero. He's a man in whom egoism dwells irreducibly, and who opposes the perfidious and authoritarian egoism of the religious priests who command him to kill and be killed.

See what his morality makes of him: an autonomous being.

He is isolated. Right. But that, you moralists, is your fault.

And then, think of the enormity that would result if this individual were to multiply in every land, becoming the majority...

*
**

The dogmatic morality is necessarily a morality that came from a religious philosophy; it's the religious morality of rights and duties.

The libertarian morality of individualism is the true scientific morality; it's the irreligious morality of pleasure, advantage, and power.

it is only natural for man to be inspired, prior to taking action, by these three motives, which, in the final analysis, boil down to pure self-interest. We are, therefore, in full harmony with nature.

In these subversive observations, our grave moralistic spectacles will only see scandal, but that hardly matters. For those of us who don't covet any of the public "cheese", it's better for us to be as honest as possible, to openly say what the hypocrites secretly think and to do, in broad daylight, what they do behind closed doors, in an idiotic shame about their own nature, even when done without any self-interested, deceitful and deceptive goal.

This is accelerated evolution, running full bore. It is true that the task of the realist brings him no monetary reward, and that he runs a strong risk of missing his chance to be a hired martyr, like so many good apostles. This is why so few take it on. But everyone envisions joy through the lenses of their own temperament. All the worse for those who find it exclusively in the belly — and even further down the abdomen; they are incomplete. Still others find it in their brains. This is how we also do the works of the egoist, by kicking idols over, to show the naive — the "poires",[4] as Parisians put it — what the idols have inside: the same appetites and the same passions as the idolaters...

***

The prejudices joined to the idea of egoism have made it into the opposite of goodness. I've already said how mistaken this view is, and explained what priestly interests lead to it. To be sure, real human interests cannot reside in the pain of others. Instead, observation teaches us that, as far as they shrug off the chains which hinder his activity, in the free play of his egoism, man would prefer to see joy in others as well as in himself. Also, isn't it only insane, sick,

---

[4] (Translator): Literally "pears": i.e. chumps, dupes.

and degenerate people who feel the abnormal desire to do evil for the pleasure in doing it? Mr. de Sade is not generally considered a paragon of health...

But again, two causes can drive man, in the absence a mature sensibility holding him back, to harm others: economic necessity — and religious sectarianism or fanaticism.

We might expect, if our brains aren't hardened like those of a moralist, that when constraints are lifted, man will no longer commit evil since nothing will oblige him to do it any longer. But, in the unlikely case where, in a free environment where forces are balanced, an individual might try to do evil for his own gratification, then his concern for own interests would restrain him, since the only outcome he could expect would be retaliation, all the more so since no law would exist to protect and privilege him such as we now have. This amounts to saying that along with laws, authoritarian institutions, and slaves, these supports of the governmental order, — the possibilities for wretched deeds would be abolished.

And so it is unnecessary to dogmatically moralize man to avoid evil. There is no need to mold him in the direction of a dogmatic goodness which, as soon as he assimilates it, turns into hatred and weakness. A secure life, economic welfare, that is, physical liberty on one side, and science in every brain, that is, intellectual and moral liberty on the other, — add to the total strength, power given to everyone, this is the fertile soil where goodness will blossom.

Let no one expect their own happiness from others. Let them be its artisan for themselves. But for this, men must be both powerful and free at the same time. Only knowledge can give them strength and liberty. For him, knowledge is what needs to be grafted onto nature, not morality. The latter comes afterwards of its own accord, as we normally conceive it: as a result — and a personal one.

Therefore, I do not repudiate goodness. Far from it, I only want it to become an egoistic necessity, the praise of life flowing from a satisfied, joyous egoism. But the practice of free and natural goodness, egoistic satisfaction, cannot be assimilated with the fulfillment of duty, the sacrifice of artificial altruism.

At most, it might be of use in educationally producing a love of life in the individual's mind, so that life (along with joy, which generates an always higher and longer existence, as a good thing, — and shortening and shrinking pain, as bad) should be, as it were, the criterion of goodness to guide slower minds through the flurry of human activity, all of which are equal in nature. The moral and social value of an act might thus be commensurate with the quantity of life it either creates and preserves or destroys, that is, by the joy or pain which it precedes. And by this benchmark, which, moreover, is interpreted according to his feelings, the individual would calibrate his relations with others, considered as associates, indifferent, or adversarial.

***

It would be very important to preserve the natural, purely realistic, and egoistic character of this criterion, as I've already pointed out. It would be important not to imprint an absolute character on it, nor to *consecrate* its object, otherwise we would end by creating a new series of duties for ourselves.

But if life is not *sacred*, I can still love it in a completely relative sense, in a certain person who is dear or useful to me. I can protect the life of my friend if I find an affective interest there, the life of my partner if I find an economic interest there, etc. Finally, more generally, I can determine the subjective value of the acts of each individual and judge according to my attitude about them, without considering said attitude as some kind of right or duty. Thus, the reason for my attitude would still be egoistic; I can, for example, judge that the acts of someone who carried out a huge massacre constitute an ongoing threat to my life and lead me to act towards him in a corresponding manner, — and inversely, with respect to a certain scientist who improves my life through all the use I can make of his discoveries.

A typical example of the danger in considering life as sacred, since it is not so in nature, nor will it ever be for the strong, — a typical example which I will never cease to talk about, since it contains a powerful lesson: the original attitude of the Doukhobors, which led a great number of them directly to death, out of their respect for life per se, Life, — a simple modality of Christian resignation.

Were the lives of the Doukhobors sacred for the Cossacks whom the Tsar sent against them? No, obviously not. But the lives of the Cossacks was sacred for the Doukhobors. The harmful character of the dogma in question rises, obviously, from observing its effects.

The same conflict appears everywhere in different guises, with robust natural consciousness on one side and artificial weakness on the other.

To say that life is sacred according the grounds that you are weak, is, as paradoxical as it may seem, making a fool's deal with the strong.

Wouldn't it have been better for the Doukhobors to have told their priests:

"Thou shalt not kill, said the teacher of resignation nineteen centuries ago. Granted. But then let nobody try to kill us, or even diminish our lives by depriving us of our liberty. Let the murderers try!"

Sure, if they said this, they wouldn't be Doukhobors any longer.

I've chosen an extreme example, but it's an easy one to relate to daily events.

Here is the definition of the individual's attitude to others in the individualistic morality. Delivered from the religious tares and the social chains, he will be good, but it will be a goodness without weakness.

You don't have to be a Christian to apply the maxim: "Do not unto others as you would not have them do unto you." For that, all it takes is to be a wise and conscious egoist. But this negative formula must be completed by this positive one: *Act towards others as the other acts towards you.*

Here is the cornerstone of the libertarian morality of individualism, a morality of realistic reciprocity and solidarity, a morality of *egoistic justice*.

V: THE EGOIST'S JUSTICE. THE INDIVIDUAL'S STRENGTH

I think I've demonstrated that no duty is imposed on man by nature: that, at birth, he is the object of no vocation, that he has no mission to fulfill, and finally, that he is ruled by only one reality: the instinct to live, which will be all the more favorable to him as he more passionately seeks to embrace his object: life.

These ideas have been said before, I'm not the first to formulate them; however, for the most part, the slaves of today, as in the past, seem to cherish their chains. They're the ones who, in concert with the masters whose force reduced them to slavery, claim that the attitude to which the performance of individualistic concepts would lead — an attitude which, if generally adopted, would actually lead to the sovereignty of the individual over himself — would favor the "ignoble reign of force", to the prejudice of that, noble beyond doubt, of "law".

Yeah, Demos, that's the ticket!

Having revealed the mechanism of duty, uncovered the aims by which this machine is set in motion and for which it works, it's important now to demolish the deceptive fiction of "law" which aims at the same goals.

Law[5]! You must be joking! We have faculties of law, professors of law, doctors and students in law. What a joke!

But, *distinguo*, these superior institutions and men are consecrated to the worship of "positive law". For there's law and then there's law!

Positive law is dreamed up by the force of ruse to justify its attacks on weakness. To despoil the laborer is not an act of triumphal force: it's an act of the purest law... The science of positive law teaches the procedure. And it's for the cultivation of this precious science that the faculties are created and the above-mentioned professors, doctors, and students are brought into existence.

A large factory owner daily makes off with the near-complete benefit of his workers' labor, tossing a pittance their way, which will let them slowly die of hunger, fatigue, alcoholism and tuberculosis; the large factory owner is neither an assassin nor a robber; he's a good, law-abiding man...

A poor man, one of the workers which the factory-owner has *used* takes back a fragment of... the legal

---

[5] (Translator): Throughout this section, note that the French word *droit* is the equivalent of both "right" and "law".

deduction which he gets from the product of his labor: he's a thief, he's working outside the laws...

Positive law is expressed by the law-code. The laws, like all the rest of the social system, are elaborated for a single purpose: keeping the strong in power, that is, in the present day, to protect property, private wealth, and capitalist theft, even to the detriment of life. For property finds its origin in force, it is preserved by force, and it reproduces force for the benefit of the proprietor.

Listen to Proudhon: "Property is theft."

Listen to Sismondi: "Most of the costs of the social establishment aim at defending the rich against the poor, because, if they were left to their respective forces, the former might soon be despoiled."

Conclude by remembering that the State has for its avowed mission to protect weakness against strength and to dispense justice. Conclude, and you will see that its real mission cannot be said aloud.

Nor should we forget that the proletariat is the majority, by which the State might not exist. Since the State is supposedly meant to establish law in society, it soon becomes plain how important it is to show the proletariat what sort of lies the fiction of law is based on, since in reality it's force that presides over the actions, both natural and social, of man.

The law is currently in the service of property. But property is only one of the present forms of authority and may, no less under the collectivist regime, give way to a single form of authority: representative authority (which is, often, not far from a pure, directorly kind of authority), just as, for example, military leaders, judges, etc., now wield it. Positive law will be at the service of tomorrow's masters, as it is today at the service of today's, if the slaves of today allow it tomorrow, and it will be perpetuated as long as the slaves concede the existence of law, and thereby consent to their own enslavement.

*
**

To positive law, "natural rights" are eagerly opposed.

What then is a natural right?

According to its priests, it's The Law — and it's a metaphysical fiction whose unreality is betrayed by the facts at every moment.

The Law is a meaningless word, since there is no instance, either in nature or society, in which the conventionally invoked law has ever been respected, has ever triumphed, if it were not backed up by power, by force. The law, then, has no only a potential value, whose realization in the act is subject to circumstances, to eventualities; therefore, it doesn't exist in any absolute sense, there is no "Law" *per se*, in the sense in which we've been taught from childhood up to understand the idea — a false one.

In the struggles of peoples, what were the Gauls' rights when faced with Roman might, the rights of the Arabs and the Malagasy before the power of the French, the rights of the Kaffirs before the power of the Boers, the rights of the Boers faced with English power, the rights of the Chinese against the combined forces of Europe, America, and Japan?

What are the rights of the minority when faced with the power of the majority, the rights of the soldier compared with the power of this leader, the rights versus the strength of the rich?

"The rights of the poor is an empty phrase."

And let us not forget that Pottier, the author of *The Internationale*, a man of a realistic and sincere proletarian mentality, and with life experience, — a painful life, — preceded it with this verse from this other:

"No duty is imposed on the rich."

What, essentially, are the rights of the weak versus the power of the strong?

Nothing at all.

And note that the strong never appeals to strength, but likewise to the law. The strong, knowing full well that the weak — the weak of the future — wouldn't voluntarily accept the effects of strength, as avowed by that generation of the strong, have always basked in the sun of their rights.

It's by means of the law invoked by those whom the tyrants and blind mobs who worked for their masters have conquered by force. Individuals, taken in isolation, act the same way.

Thus the Bismarckian slogan: "Strength is above law" would be true and excellent in its terms, as a statement of fact, if law actually resided anywhere besides the nebulous regions of metaphysics. It's a product of the human imagination which can't reasonably be juxtaposed with the reality of strength.

If we wish to consider in the law's capacity for action, its power to do things, we must conclude that *the law is constituted only by strength.*

But in this case... why even talk about laws?

Law, then, is also a phantom which evaporates in the light of reason.

Let's now banish law and rights from our mentality, just as we drove out duty. And let us become strong by replacing them with *my* liberty, *your* liberty, *their* liberty, — or, as might be more intelligible in the present state of the human mentality, *my* will, *your* will, *their* will.

*
**

Individualism, a realistic, truthful conception, ignores rights as well as duties and only thinks about interests and wills served by forces. "Be strong if you want to be free", it tells mankind.

Thus the proletarians, — the current crop of the weak, by virtue of the ignorance all around them, — by recognizing the existence of the law, are falling for the same trick as when they recognize the sanctity of life.

They have nothing to expect from the masters of proprietary authority or from those of representative authority. Quibbling over the law is wasted time, that is, wasted life. They will never have the law on their side as long as they show weakness. If they want emancipation and satisfaction, it will only happen when they become strong and put this strength to work in the service of their interests — their common interests.

Right and duty, in a system of liberty, of anarchy, would allow for conventions between individuals or associations. The individuals might, if they wish to use such terms, recognize each other's duties and rights, but, in our strictly utilitarian, relative, and variable sense, which is rooted in voluntary obligation and remuneration, how far these words would be from the meanings they hold in the religious mindset! This free and effectively contractual justice, which varies with individuals and groupings, with interests and affinities, has its point of departure in the individual, in each self, and submits to it. Those individuals who practice this relative justice would not be any kind of devotees of Justice, they would be free men establishing an always mutable egoistic justice.

An original collective act of egoistic justice is what will lead to the overturning of capitalistic society, when the proletarians will finally have understood and applied this idea which Max Stirner suggests to them in this immense book of human truth which is *The Ego and Its Own*: "the workers have a formidable power; when they finally realize this and decide to use it, nothing will be able to resist them: all they will need to do is to cease all labor and appropriate all its products, these products of their labor which they would see as theirs since they made them[6]."

Refractory against the compulsion of duty and unhindered by the deceptive confidence in law, then the individual becomes capable of liberty, for he is aware of his strength. He can develop without fear in the midst of forces, whether partnered or adversarial. But we have no reason to believe that, in an

---

[6] (Translator): From Part I, "Man", Section: "Political Liberalism".

environment where this wisdom is understood and lived out, that there will even be adversarial forces, since antagonism could only arise from two causes which will have disappeared along with authority: fanaticism and economic malaise. The enlightened self-interest of each egoism changes things so that only associated forces will exist. Competition is harmonized. Men have become fit for individualistic association.

VI: INDIVIDUALISTIC ASSOCIATION

The object of the present study is to give a glimpse into the (as yet imperfectly formulated) doctrine of libertarian individualism, and especially to demonstrate that, contrary to the prejudice which represents the individualist as being opposed to all agreement with others and all association, the practical consequence of the individualist philosophy is association, but a previously unparalleled kind of association, in which each partner will have neither the temptation nor the possibility of "rolling over" the others. The reader will already have noticed, from my analysis of the individual and his relations with others, that the association of men liberated from rights and duties is conceivable, and will recognize that this kind of association should logically be the goal of the efforts of intelligent men. It remains for me to give as precise a theoretical idea, as possible, of what this association would look like.

***

The capitalist society which we presently suffer is a form of authoritarian, anti-individualistic association, in which solidarity is compulsory (which explains why J. H. Mackay considers it communistic), as revealed by all the social institutions: legislative, judicial, proprietary, military, national, and so on. Due to the logomachy of the political parties, the collectivists regard it as individualistic by virtue of the false acceptation of the word "individualism", discussed at the beginning of this study, and they carefully avoid adding its complementary qualification: "authoritarian" or "bourgeois", since that would consecrate a distinction where they have an interest in promoting confusion.

In this society, you pay yourself — or rather you are paid — above all in words: there, the citizens are free, equal, sacred, voters, eligible, fraternized into orders, what else? But none of that keeps the great majority of these citizens from stagnating in an ignoble slavery or keeps many of them from collapsing from starvation for the higher profits of the lazy privileged, whose property (property is theft) in capital and its interest is guaranteed by the State (the just redistributor!), which property, however, originates from the labor of the usurping capitalist's employees.

The death of a society like this is sanctioned, which its proletarians will execute as soon as they are *strong* enough.

Collectivistic society is another form of authoritarian association, likewise anti-individualist, whose solidaristic constraints would present themselves in different guises, of course, but which would exist no less. Its yoke might make itself felt in a less ferocious way: there, it one might be paid less in words and more in subsistence, but in it one would probably still suffer from parasites.

Might we elude the collectivistic period and pass directly to individualistic association? Or are we destined by the very nature of our evolution to know the decadent yoke of collectivism? This is a secret for tomorrow. This second hypothesis, though, seems more likely. In this case, our interest would be expressed in the wish for its realization soon, — whose advent, besides, seems to have been prepared by capitalism itself in organic endeavors, — for this society would have this excellent feature for individuals aspiring to autonomy, that its authoritarian cadres and wheels would be relatively weak and easy to break, and that it would prepare the organizations of production, exchange and consumption for the moment of true liberation, which are preconditions of individualistic association.

Any victory of collectivism over capitalism would simply attest a desire for emancipation, which would have moved the proletariat in an imperfect way. In this sense, and even if it allowed parasites to remain, realized collectivism would mark a stage in the path towards the only ideal capable of being subjected to the individual, representing exactly his social thing, and whose thing he can never become: individualistic association, — the "association of egoists".

*
**

We've seen that individualism is clearly opposed to the obligatory association which the State of today imposes and which the State of tomorrow will impose, but it accepts, or rather, its very own is freely contracted association between individuals. It pits free association against obligatory association. The individualist refuses to serve the association considered as an end, or to sacrifice any part of his individuality to the illusory interest of the association, — a socialistic and authoritarian principle. But he wants the association to serve him, he himself, the individual considered as an end; he wants to employ it according to his real interests, — an individualistic and libertarian principle. In sum, association is a means of life for him, and not the point of his life.

With socialism, the religion of Society (the capitalistic socialism of today, which is a cynical expression of the enslaving selfishness of our proprietary bourgeoisie — or the collectivistic socialism of tomorrow, which is the veiled expression of the same enslaving selfishness of the new bourgeoisie, when the representatives have changed into directors), the individual is sacrificed, in the name of a so-called general or collective interest which is utterly illusory, to the interest of the owners or directors, the masters, the strong: in brief, the powerful.

He has to become as strong and powerful as them; all he'll need is to have an active will to become such; then he will be his own master, to gain self-mastery, and, in addition, when a similar attitude becomes generalized, harmony will be established in society.

Under the socialist regime (capitalist or collectivist), encouraged by the priests of the religious idea of Society, the prosperity of the association is the purpose of the individual's life, the individual's life is a means for the association. The profiteers are always backstage.

With libertarian individualism, the individual, irreligious at last, no longer has to sacrifice himself to association, since he only participates in it according to his wants and needs. The prosperity of his life is the goal of his association, his association is the means for his life. The profiteers would disappear.

The sacrifice of the individual to the phantom called "Society" is obtained by a bluff which requires a total idiocy from its victim: it consists in the "subordination of particular interests to the general interest".

The general interest — an abstraction — should never clash with particular interests, whose precise expression it must be in a well-organized world; but in this case it would be useless to invoke such a thing. The general interest is therefore a lie: there are only particular interests. But let us grant its existence for the moment. So, there is a difference between the so-called general interest, invoked to obtain the sacrifice of the individual — and his own interest. The proof of this truth is in the fact that the moralists teach men to "see past their own small circle", and that they come right out and say that "the good citizen should subordinate his personal interest to the general interest" (the interest of Society, of the Fatherland, etc.). But consider what this "general interest" conceals: the particular interests of masters, of their priests, and other associations of valets within the State. The State is nothing but a ridiculous church where Masses are said in favor of "collective reason", the State is also an "association of malefactors"...

Every time your personal interest differs from the general interest which is raised against you, and to which they want you to sacrifice yourself, proletarians, you should check to see which parasites are benefiting by said difference: translated into money, it goes into their bank accounts...

*
**

Finally, there is no need to focus on what no well-informed person ever questions, i.e.: that man is a naturally sociable animal, not only because of moral and sentimental needs, but also physical, economical and intellectual ones. There's no point repeating what everybody knows: that association multiplies human enjoyments while reducing their burdens.

As much through rational interest as through instinctive tendency, association presents itself to the individual as a larger and higher way to live.

Individualist wisdom will not make anyone repudiate the principle of association on the pretext that, up to now, the senses were denatured, but, on the contrary, it will incite them to organize their associations such that it should be their thing and they can't be sacrificed in the name of this thing to the interests of others.

FEMININE INDIVIDUALITY

1914

People typically talk about the constitution of human individuality as if two categories of human beings didn't exist or, when they do mention this duality, they discuss it as if their interests were always identical by nature. This is far true: the interests of female individuals are not exactly the same as those of male individuals. These interests are necessarily similar as far as the sexes are biologically similar, but as concerns the sexual life, they are so distinct that, if they sometimes line up artificially, thanks to the intelligence of the interested parties, they most often appear in utterly antagonistic forms: such is the case when the sexual partners have let blind nature free to govern their relations — i.e., in most cases.

Therefore, anyone who would resolve the problem of the sovereignty of the individual over himself, no longer the inner life only, but in social life as well, and in those rudimentary forms of society which are the couple and the family, must look at the constitution of feminine individuality differently than the masculine one.

From this preamble it will be understood that I'm talking about a libertarian individualism with a universalizing tendency, and not about a bourgeois or authoritarian pseudo-individualism, which only means to legitimize the attacks of the strong against the weak, attacks which are daily facts in sexual life. The so-called individualist who's an authoritarian has no problem making this distinction between the interests of men and women, but would rather the public not know about it: he's only in service to the strong. Thus, he solves the problem by insincerely confusing these two categories of interests, thus smashing the weaker party. I.e., he sacrifices the individuality of the woman to that of the man. And while doing so, he does not lack for sophisms: he's satisfied to place it in the perspective of the interests or illusory will of any suitable "phantom": Family, Society, Country, Race, Humanity, Nature, God, and so on.

The reasoning of a sensible individualist aims not at exacerbating the existing antagonism between two individuals who have to live in association, but at finding the conditions which might create harmony between them, a peace requiring no sacrifice from either party. Their divergent interests only lose their value when the strong is trying to dominate the weak, at which time the individuality of the individualist which is threatened is the only one that matters.

Yet, aside from the noble exceptions I've envisioned while sketching out the neo-Malthusian family[7] arranged according to love or justice, which individual in human couples is most frequently oppressed by their partner, but the woman, — who is the plainly weaker of the two by virtue of nature, and of whose situation is only made worse by the social organization, which has never been anything but the systematic reproduction of natural inequality and injustice.

When Neo-Malthusianism crosses from economics to ethics, it defends women's sexual liberty. In fact, with its practical means, it gives them a powerful element, constitutive of their individuality, to the extent that this depends on sexual activity. Rather than that soporific feminism of the prudish moralists or those who aspire to a politician's salary and other parasites, it is the primordial, if not the only tool, of her emancipation from masculine guardianship. Since her inferiority in the struggle for life is due to her sex, her sex, which puts her at the mercy of the male's whim, a conscientious feminist, an intelligent woman will always prefer an obstructive pessary over the stupid voters' rags...

*
**

It's the custom, for plenty of mock skeptics who add paradoxical expressions to old-fashioned French gallantry, — the complete hypocrisy, — to say that man is pitifully weak versus woman. If we take them

---

[7] *The Neo-Malthusian Family.*

at their word, women are forever abusing their natural ascendancy to make a plaything of their men.

I don't deny that this does happen. But I have to add that, when it comes to humanity in general, such cases are very rare.

In reality, when a man seems oppressed by a woman who takes advantage of the fact that she's to his taste, and makes him pay for the privilege, whether legitimate or otherwise, of her charms at an exorbitant rate or makes him do otherwise painful things, this is because the man is a slave to his own sexuality: and he pays dearly, in money or favors, for the satisfaction of a taste, a passion, a compelling need which imposes itself tyrannically, and which he either knows not how or simply can't resist.

We should rather consider those who seem to love paradox and over-generalization as discerning minds, and their affirmations of women's power as a clever way of hiding from eyes of women, which tend to be myopic, real life, which is the exact opposite. This is closely related to the hypocrisy of the lazy and the social parasites, which circulates in dithyrambs about the nobility of labor and the sanctity of the laborer, which allows them alone, as the priests of this faith, to do nothing and still live the good life.

When they declare the omnipotence of woman, our professors of illusion give license to man to treat her as the instrument of a pleasure whose costs will be paid for with all her births or abortions. Besides which, they induce the woman to doze in the vanity of an illusory royalty, until she wakes up one day, too late, finally aware that she's been tricked in the sexual association. It's long since these good sirs have kept us looking at feminine ruses. And the masculine? But they're no more men than Mr. Josse was a jeweler!

This is the gentle way. It contains several varieties. The clichés about the greatness of woman's mission, about her eminent role in the family, society, and humanity, come under this modality of deceit. Even the pains of pregnancy and childbirth and the drudgery of slavery which are called the "joys of motherhood" by our moralists, — insincere, all of them! No man aspiring to the title of an altruist could ever deprive his wife of these joys, and the most meritorious is he who gives them to her most often! Thus, masculine altruism flows up to the banks...

But what! Are these degradations of the ideal not the norm with the masters, who indulge in them in order to mislead their subjects on the nature of the required tasks, which, if reason had priority in their brains, they wouldn't carry out of their own accord?

Doubtless, for a small number of women, you can't deny that there's some reality in that. No more than you can claim that in some distant day, when human individuality, and especially the feminine one, will no longer count for anything, such things would not exist. But today, with our barbaric social organization, in the present state of morals and the common mentality, these clichés don't generally correspond with the facts: motherhood, when imposed by the man's authority on the woman's ignorance or weakness, — when he hasn't made her have an abortion, — only brings pain and servitude. But, false as they are, these poetic lies continue to nurture, even with help from the feminists, the sexual slavery of woman.

*
**

The truth about the sexual relations is less pretty than all the fictions beneath which men hide it. That's only one more reason to unveil it. I won't say: when she gets out of the well, for she zealously covers the opening, but when, in the bottom of the well which is the masculine soul, the psychologist goes searching for it, he sees her as follows.

With the exception, among men, of those who think and act completely like Neo-Malthusians, for some, the prolific brutes who are driven by a fixed idea or their whim, or also leaders in search of fodder for cannons and labor, the woman is a womb which is *fortunately* preceded by a vagina; for the rest, who essentially have no interest in the ballooning of abdomens, but in whom there is neither love nor that pity which can generate salutary measures for women, she's a vagina *unfortunately* followed by a womb.

But, whether he rejoices or frets about the structure of women's genital apparatus, the result is the same: under his domination, she is no longer anything, to use Proudhon's phrase, but a "machine for reproduction", which that uncomprehending anti-Malthusian, a ferocious anti-feminist and anarchist by turns found otherwise perfect. He especially favored in the strong way. "Whore or housewife", was the dilemma he offered woman. To the housewives he naturally annexed the job of being a machine for reproduction, through which, ultimately, being a machine for pleasure is also apparent. Thus, his housewife has a similar life to that of the whore, on the bad side.

Oh! We may smile at the naivety of abbé Violet, who, at a Neo-Malthusian meeting, shared his view that the only sexual morality worthy of being practiced was the traditional one, which issued from Christianity and which "refuses to make woman into an instrument for enjoyment".

O chaste — I like to think so — but incompetent abbé, by the absurd prohibitions of your morality, by its contempt for everything good in nature, and by its hatred of free thinking, which is the only thing which can, for the betterment of humanity, help them adapt to the natural laws, — your morality makes of woman, not only an instrument of enjoyment, but above all an instrument of painful enjoyment: a beast for pleasure, a beast for suffering, following the impulses of the male whom "God made in his image". But, as ever-fluctuating Proudhon said, in this case speaking as a true anarchist: "God is evil"; and, for the goodness of life, man must surpass himself, i.e., surpass your "God".

It hardly matters that, in the game of love, men or women find a means of pleasure in their partner, if neither of them suffer for it, but things are different in the practice of Christian morality, even in its disguise called "secular morality".

May liberty have free rein, unless it brings avoidable pain!

*
**

Every man in whom a refined sensibility vibrates is anguished by the thought of any suffering which he might inflict on others as a mere byproduct of the life in him. He tries to minimize the effects of the destructive power which he and all other living creatures have. True, he vigorously refuses to be anyone's victim, but nor does he victimize anyone else. Above all, with respect to the weak creature who is his companion, the eventuality of consecutive pregnancies arising from coitus troubles his mind; he resolves the matter to the satisfaction of both concerns, without sacrificing either of them, for his is raised from the physical plane to the moral plane.

Pity, though! Such men are relatively rare. This will continue for a long time, maybe forever. If they were numerous, social life would change its aspect. Let's not count too much on the accession of man to super-humanity. Let's not put our trust entirely in the good will of the strong. Let's leave these fragile hopes to the religions, while their hopes are not yet realized, this honeyed trick, the poison consciously poured on those who are now weak, forever deadening the potential energy dormant in them. Let's fight the master's charity with the revolt of the slaves, with is much more effective. Let's give woman the enlightenment of sexual truths and the defensive weapons to assure her victory against her male oppressor: we'll have contributed massively to the realization of her individuality.

Against authoritarians of every ilk, whether the deprived or the leaders, who keep their wives the way they like her, speaking as an individualist and a Neo-Malthusian, I say to the eternal sacrificial victim: "Live your life, woman, not the one man imposes on you. Be yourself at last and not some wavering thing. It's intolerable to the existence of a human being, whatever their sex, to be at the mercy of another who has a quasi-right of property, in the utter fullness of this right: to use and abuse what he owns. It is inadmissible for an individual, i.e. a woman, not to be the absolute master of their body and that another, i.e. a man, to, by whim or surprise, be able to modify this body, placing it in jeopardy of death or degeneration, and, as often as he likes, grafting an external life onto it. Pregnancy must only come with the woman's consent. When a man tells you that it's impossible for coitus not to lead to pregnancy, he's lying. It's always possible. You must defend yourself against an individual like that. Practical Neo-Malthusianism has the means which will put you almost entirely beyond the reach of any attempts at undesired fertilization, and your partner doesn't need to know."

Let no man then raise the objection: "This will be the destruction of the human couple, it's the death of the family!" In the sociological mode I'm in, I pay no attention to metaphysics. Instead of an entity called The Couple, I see a man and a woman: two physical people; instead of the entity called A Family, I see a father, a mother, and children: so many real beings. If, with respect to their modes of association, couples and families are founded on oppression, then I don't give a damn if they are reduced, or even vanish. But the result of woman's acquisition of a safeguard against male sexual tyranny will be quite different: masculine strength will come to terms with the new feminine strength, it's as simple as that.

To the man I would respond: "So you don't want to be a companion, but a master? You want your companion to be your slave, submissive to your good will, even when it's murderous? Doesn't she also have a right to individuality? If you deny this to her, it will like be due to your strength, which prudently hides behind sophisms: so, it's only logical for her to make herself strong. By virtue of nature, your interests are opposed on some points; but it's a task for your rational mind to surpass nature and, by compromising, to harmonize your divergent interests. If both of you, and especially you yourself, have carried out this wise task: if, ultimately, your interests can be identified, then how, from the fact that your companion wants live her life, that is, shows a desire to be herself, should this lead to any misunderstanding between you, given that your respective lives would then go along in parallel? In a state of harmony, when each lives their own life, they live the other's also. Without similar rational agreement, there will only be struggle between you: abuse and violence on one side, and subterfuge from your companion, either that or abject resignation. Our enemy is our master. In that case you are your companion's enemy, and I would be overjoyed to bring a moral divorce to you, even a real divorce, if, as a supporter of feminine individualism, practical Neo-Malthusianism doesn't make this divorce pointless. Through the power it gives to women who live in a miserable sexual association, it tempers the war of the sexes from the smile of those who were weak just prior, but now hold the secret weapon by which all liberticidal ambitions are crushed."

THE NEO-MALTHUSIAN FAMILY

1914

From the first day of sexual association — whether in marriage or a free union — a life is confided to man.

I say *confided*, because this association isn't a contract in which the respective parties have equal power, and each has guarantees of their own. If we look for a contract here, we can only find an unfavorable contract there, since the natural law governing this association has already, *per se*, guaranteed the woman's oppression by the man, and the social law only intervenes to guide and organize this oppression by placing public power at the service of masculine authority.

For women, the most tangible form of slavery comes in the form of motherhood. It's not hard to see that, by her weakness with respect to man and due to the processes of copulation and conception, woman falls into the hands of a prolific brute (whose bestial nature can also present itself to her with successive full-term pregnancies or sequential abortions), if this woman fails to defend herself, she will suffer a slavery whose chains will always heavier and always more tightly fastened, and which will only end with her annihilation in suffering.

In sexual association, then, which factors will bring liberty to woman, a liberty which can coexist with that of man, on condition, definitely, that he doesn't seek his pleasure in the enslavement of a creature who's weaker than himself?

In cases where they've reached an understanding, these will only be of masculine origin, precisely because it's a question of the association of a weaker party, woman, who's especially fit for receiving, and of a stronger party, man, fitted to give. In cases where they're fighting[8], the only possible factor will obviously originate with the woman, and will consist in her self-defense.

But here I'm not only looking, as my title indicates, only at cases of mutual understanding.

Among these elements of liberty, first is the man's love, a love made of insightful comprehension and receptive sensibility, — true love, which is an elevated egoism, in which the other's interests are as dear to you as your own, and not the absorbing and more or less sadistically destructive passion for the so-called beloved. If this great love burns in the man's heart, he will be careful about his woman's body, the health or

---

[8] See *Feminine Individuality*.

decline of which will be reflected in his own morale, as joy or pain.

However, if, without dissolving the association, friendship, even indifference, takes the place of love, a spirit of justice can make up the difference; but here it's a matter of a justice which exists neither in nature nor in society and which only the individual, situating himself above such things, can wish to realize on his own account.

These are the solid bases for a possible association between a strong and a weak party, wherein each of them has the guarantee — completely intuitive with the weaker party and yet well grounded — not fall victim to the other. The association of these candidates for super-humanity is what makes them a Neo-Malthusian couple.

If neither love nor justice are present, the last chance for the woman's liberty is when the man is open to a longer-term economic interest, in the suggestion of prudence in procreation, — which is a rather uncertain thing, for this interest will have no place, for example, if the man is wealthy.

Outside these three determinatives of man's feelings for woman, nothing remains for her but oppression from the sexual point of view and, consequently, from several other points of view, — unless she is manages to defend herself against the male.

For the ordinary man, isn't a woman, *his woman*, a creature whom, even in the absence of society's legal consecration and the Church's sacrament, nature has put into his power, and given him the definitive right to slowly destroy her for his own enjoyment?

To keep the sexual association from ending in this destruction of the weak by the strong, which is deliberate and intentional to some extent, by successive pregnancies or abortions, the stronger party must be sufficiently evolved and have brought his reason and feelings a few hundred cubits above the moral — and amoral — realm of the gorillas of our humanity.

He who lacks strength, indeed, lacks rights, objective rights, the only ones that matter, — meanwhile, the value of the other, their subjective rights, are a matter for the stronger one's conscience, constituting a gift to the weak.

Now, Neo-Malthusianism doesn't count only on this good will: it provides the woman with a means of defense; but for the moment I'm speaking as if she were initially unaware of these means, and where the association goes along peacefully and not in war.

In practice, the libertarian and Neo-Malthusian individualistic idea of a tacit contract suited to harmonious regulation of sexual association will beat back the darker forces of nature and society, replacing the worst aspects of this contract with respect by the strong for the liberty of the weak.

It influences man in such a way as to induce a supreme pity in him, which resolves itself in abstention from inflicting any perilous, painful, or undesired pregnancy on his companion. By its effect on the woman, it gives her that strength which grants the individual full awareness of a right, even a purely subjective one, — in the species, her right to be a mother only with her consent, that of being the single and supreme arbiter of her person.

*
**

Therefore, at the threshold of all sexual association, a weakness is at the mercy of a strength.

How will the Neo-Malthusian man behave: the completely Neo-Malthusian man, i.e., he who sees higher and further in life than the economic angle, which embraces the moral side no less, since he lives no less internally than externally; an individualist, ultimately, who defends not only his own right to individuality?

The moralists have said and repeated to him that, from the moment he "started a family", new duties devolved upon him, among which is that of producing a numerous posterity.

Some have taught him to fulfill this duty to Society, by enlarging the number of producers; to his Country, by giving it more defenders; to God or Nature, by reproducing to perpetuate the species, etc.

My Neo-Malthusian only smiles: he knows what people mean when they invoke these eminent personalities, whose greatest merit for him is that they are only ghosts, scarecrows intended to shoo away those who would have access if they weren't afraid of ghosts. He isn't unaware that morality is an invention of the moralists intended to yoke, to the caprice or interests of their masters, individuals who would otherwise live according to personal principles. And since, if, the as a generous stronger party, he willingly and spontaneously gives something to his beloved weaker party, he wants any duty that's invoked to demand anything from to result from a contract and correspond to a real right; and yet, he has signed no contract with any dignitary, and he would seek in vain for any corresponding right that they might grant him.

Some have attributed other reasons for this duty. They say that he's fulfilling his duty to his wife, who only married him for the sake of motherhood, and it would be an insult not to prolifically fertilize her; to himself as well, since, for his own honor and under penalty of being called a eunuch, prove his virility.

My Neo-Malthusian has no fear of adjectives; he knows the value of words, and he fights them with these great antidotes: contempt and irony. He has also had reason to smile, the incorrigible skeptic! But he knows what duties he really contracted as far as his companion is concerned, from the start. She, too, besides, for in the Neo-Malthusian couple, the woman has a voice in the matter: she is no longer simply the inseminated female. These duties truly result from a freely negotiated contract between them and, unfortunately for the moralists and their teachers, they're totally different from what these people respect. Principal among them, for the man, is never to make his companion a mother without her consent. Along with a duty to himself: never to act like a brute.

No doubt, here is something to shock the cretins and scumbags of holy Morality. But my Neo-Malthusian is an evolved man. His education began with his grandparents, when the sperm and the egg from which he would come still existed only in potential, in the two other sperms and two other eggs. He's the product of two generations who are sufficiently educated in the ways of liberty and responsibility so that the third can be fully cognizant of such things. The moralist has no more power over an individual who was reconstituted so long before he ever came into the world.

He is aware of the weakness of this woman who is confided to him. He would feel terrified by the idea of deceiving the confidence of this being who, naturally and legally, is his thing. His love dictates his behavior to him, but he knows that if this feeling ever disappears, his sense of justice will make up the difference.

Fortunately, in her he finds an intelligent companion. To be sure, she didn't know much of the activities corresponding to her sex. Isn't a young girl supposed to be ignorant of all that? Her parents think for her on this matter, and will find her a son-in-law someday who will initiate her as he pleases. But, at least, she's not uptight and has been spared by God. She's unafraid of the truths her companion has to teach her. With him she understands that, in the end, the human object of the sexual association, whatever sentimentality it's draped in, is the need to maximize the safe exercise of the sexual organs of each partner. Like him, she now knows that, aiming at unknown and likely unknowable aims, — and that we humans mistaking the means for the end, and call it the perpetuation of the species, — the cosmic force lays for man, like all other animals, the trap of pleasure.

The cosmic force hardly cares — be it good and almighty God, Providence, or Good Nature, in the more naive faith — if individuals are destroyed by the assigned task, so long as offspring are the result, on whom it will impose, if she's docile enough, the same merry-go-round, which serves its purposes. But if it's not agreeable to both lovers to give satisfaction to the indifferent cosmic force, it will get no offspring; and, no more than they would have been rewarded for having produced them, they won't be punished for failing to comply.

If one of them desires a posterity and the other doesn't, no child will be born to them. He who is tempted by the idea of fatherhood knows that he doesn't have the right to impose on his companion a pregnancy to which she doesn't consent. No doubt, he could invoke the rights of his natural endowment of strength: by violence or ruse, he could get his way; but he abandons this brutish right: the rights of strength are ignoble when used to restrict the liberty or life of another; they are noble only with he who, justly, defends himself against the brute inside of him, and does what he can to neutralize it.

What is more, in cases when the legitimate desire for a reasonably-sized posterity (one child, two at most) would be too imperious for him, does he not have the right to leave the wife who cannot or will not give him this satisfaction? Aren't there other possible solutions in addition? Zola gives an example of a clever and nice solution. But shouldn't everything be arranged amicably between rational beings?

*
**

This desire, born in him, is increased.

For a Malthusian, even of the *Neo-* variety, is not necessarily someone who desires the extinction of the human species.

80

She and he are perfect, physically. Their health is good. He makes a good living and they could easily afford one or two children. Quite free, he feels quite strong and consequently responsible for his acts and their consequences.

Once, then again, he has divulged this desire with his companion and she has consented, freely and amorously, to be a mother. A boy and, a few years later, a girl are born, and both were wanted.

He realizes what a huge gift of she makes of herself in these circumstances. It's no secret that these children will be cherished. And, likewise, if she gets caught up, she called for fertility again, so that against her own will, by this spirit of sacrifice which often moves the weak when the strong having given proofs of their good intentions, or by some other irrational impulse, he would restore her to wiser paths, using his privilege of superior rationality over her.

These two children didn't ask to be born; and, later on, if they turn out miserable, they'll be right to criticize their father for having given them life. The father knows this: he would have done the same with his father, in other circumstances. It's because he knows that if, in the Neo-Malthusian sexual association, there is a contract between man and woman, especially a procreative one, with a subsequent exchange of rights and duties, things are different between the parents and the child, and with good reason. In the act of procreating, man acts with the utmost arbitrariness: he imposes, often he afflicts, by his own authority, life on a creature whom he draws from nothingness. In this way he is using a right, a terrible right, with which, *ipso facto*, comes a duty, — an imperative duty for every free and responsible man: to keep this creature from suffering.

Thus, when my Neo-Malthusian performs this act of plenary authority, he promises to make free creatures of his two children, who are rational and sufficiently armed that they won't be crushed in the struggle for life, and yet not to be ferocious beasts themselves. And yet he never talks about this duty. Because he desired these children, he loves them: he loved them before they were born. For him, this duty is mixed with his noble egoism, with his moral self-interest, and therefore he'll raise them in the finest and best way.

This father wanted a son in his own image. He would feel sadness and contempt for this son, and plenty for himself too, if he saw him acting brutishly at any time. And slowly, but surely, he raises the young man as he himself was raised: both physically and morally, without neglecting the inner being any more than the external one. He is forever sheltered, along with the unknown creature who will be his female companion one day, from the pitfalls of sexual life.

The mother, too, ever since she received her Neo-Malthusian initiation from her companion, has understood that, instead of realizing such a happy association, she might easily have been, in her ignorance, the prey of a prolific brute. The thought that her daughter might one day fall victim to another one shakes her to the core. At the appearance of certain thing, which, as normal as it may be, is new and bizarre to the young girl, her mother begins to teach her about its future role. Progressively, she puts her on guard against the dangers it entails. And the time will come when she will show her how to be a mother only when she wants to.

For these are parents who *love* their children.

*
**

This is the Neo-Malthusian family: a house of happiness and a school for happiness.

EDUCATION AND LIBERTY

1900

I.

There are some who, filled with goodwill in the libertarianism they profess, but with narrow minds, would like to reject all education, or, at least, reduce its influence over the individual to the unavoidable minimum. For them, education, an instrument of subjugation, and individuality, an expression of liberty in a human unity, are two opposed and utterly irreconcilable terms.

As if to confirm this opinion, the educational professionals, teachers and moralists, take care to surround the human mind with darkness to facilitate the enslavement of the whole person. Moreover, they're all Tartuffes assuring their voluntary victims that this education will give them liberty, of the true and unique sort, the kind of liberty which results from authority properly understood — and properly endured!

Our people of goodwill and narrow thinking owe to their simplicity the fact that they only see the harmful side of education.

But there is another side.

Education can be understood as a force.

And every force, in itself, is neutral.

It's the impressions he receives, the guidance he's given, the goal he's made to reach for, which make a force good or bad for man, depending on whether its effects are favorable or unfavorable for his nature, and whether it brings him joy or pain.

Similarly, education is good for the individual if it occurs in conditions favorable to his continual development, that is, if he's presented with individual autonomy as his target, and if the means of liberty are used to this purpose.

It is bad if it occurs in conditions which lead to the reduction or effacement of the individual, that is, if the means of authority are employed and if slavery, under any form whatsoever, is intended for the individual.

The error, then, lies in the absence of any distinction between the two kinds of education which it is possible to give to man: libertarian education and authoritarian education, — corresponding to the two great principles on which human actions are based: liberty and authority.

It is obvious that, by definition, — and analysis, as attested by experience — authoritarian education and individuality are mutually exclusive while libertarian education and individuality are in full accord.

Now, the conditions of human happiness reside largely in the quality of the *individual*, in the wholeness of his individuality. This is a philosophical truth which is too well demonstrated by libertarian thinkers to require any emphasis.

It follows that there is no better and safer way to reach for a relative happiness than the libertarian education of man.

As much as the stagnation which is encouraged and imposed by the ruling bourgeois mentality, one begins to tire of the rhetoric of those who sell utopias and those who traffic in the ideal, as well as the incitement to collective and bloody rebellion coming from certain professional revolutionaries. All of them pour out for humanity hope for the future, — hope, which puts energies to sleep. It's a sterile task, when it's not noxious. We want happiness immediately, and it's up to us, and only us, to get it for ourselves.

This is why worthy minds, who, without distinctions of class, are working for social rebirth, look for positive and immediate solutions. They agree in recognizing that it's through scientific instruction, along with an apprenticeship in moral liberty, that man will attain definitive liberation from the economic, moral and intellectual perspectives, and then, with his fellows, create a milieu of free individuals, who are rationally egoistic and committed to one another, and therefore able to make Justice bloom, a flower which is only a luxury right now.

This is a way of truly starting the libertarian social task at the beginning; it is, in the well-known expression, no longer placing the cart before the horse, like those so-called libertarians who encourage the violent revolutionary action before individuals have undergone the personal development which is indispensable if we want our social endeavor to have staying power.

In a society based on authority, Law, and public Opinion, — the latter perverted by Morality and authoritarian education — these are used to create respect for this authority and its representations. It then becomes impossible for the awakened minority to attempt any immediate realization, whether peaceful or bellicose, of a social milieu based on liberty, since all the forces of the government, along with the ignorant majority itself, stand ready to perform the task of repression, at the first sign of either destruction or construction.

The stumbling-block for every attempt to realize a libertarian society is the effects of the harmful education received from childhood up. Throughout his whole life, man bears the burden of prejudice, worship, respect, and false or incomplete information which were inculcated in him as a child. All he does is forever bound up with the monstrous mentality which was formed for him.

Those born blind have no notion of light: a little island from birth onwards, the man of today cannot comprehend liberty.

Already, in the family, the child's education occurs in an authoritarian way. Those families are extremely rare in which the father, acting intelligently, has been able to get rid of his belief in the legitimacy of paternal authority and in the full necessity of violence or coercion to make a man of his child. Few are the fathers who don't consider their child as their property, their thing, and fewer still are those who teach them to think, examine, reason, criticize, and decide with true independence.

Why is the father generally the opposite of this ideal? Why, he doesn't know, but it's obviously because he himself suffered his own father's violence and imperious will, who thus restrained, even to the bottom of his juvenile soul, any desire to love and understand life, along with his budding curiosity and affections.

The spirit of liberty, spread profusely in younger minds over the course of evolution, will sap the power of paternal authority until it is utterly annihilated in the blossoming of a milieu of justice.

For their part, the child's educators who are external to the family have been and remain strange breeders of monsters, like those people who get a kick out of mutilating animals by cutting off some of their organs or grafting extra parts on them. What the latter do to the body, the former have done to the intellect, and this wasn't for thrills, but through submission to the leaders, on whom the isolation of the ignorant, the weak, and the ill-educated confers power, profit, privilege and much else besides. This is how they have fashioned, in their sad laboratories: secular schools, church schools, or shops for those who push polluted goods, these repulsive creatures hated by all the healthy men who are left.

Thus, from now on, it's a point of agreement for all men of good faith, who know how to think and who dream of a better life, that, for this to be realized, for it to hasten the coming of a new world whose possible foundations have been pointed out by many sociologists, the education to be given to man which aims at this outcome must begin in his early youth. It is indispensable that, from the age when curiosity about existence awakens in his mind, the child should be spared lies and errors, while the path of truth is shown to him clearly.

Around eighteen is the age at which the intelligent young man begins attending meetings and conferences dealing with social education, leafing through specialized journals where he finds better intellectual fare than all the nauseating pornography, which is more substantial than the moronic stories in which enslaving prejudices are diluted and burdensome dogmas are affirmed, which make man into a machine for praying, voting, and sweating, and a beast to be killed on the battlefield, — and so, around eighteen is quite late for such an arduous task to be crowned with very brilliant results. Besides, for every one intelligent young man who stops to listen and read such things, a hundred others avoid them and only care about café-concerts, their gymnastic club, whorehouses, and the usual everyday trivialities of the masses.

As for what concerns the young intelligent man who educates himself alone and freely in the way of truth and reason, it is, let us say, quite late for the direction he gives to his thought to influence the rest of his existence very much, for it must be understood that libertarian education and integral instruction shouldn't aim only at the happiness of future humanity by aiming only at preparing for an uncertain and far-off harmonious society, but also and especially aiming at the happiness of man in contemporary society, by teaching him to live immediately and in the fullest measure possible: freely, naturally, and rationally, — a result which can only be acquired by the individual if he had been nourished on the principles of liberty, truth, and reason from the most propitious age, when the brain is most malleable and impressionable, and forever bears the marks of primary education: that is, from childhood.

For, whether he's been taught in a religious school or a secular school, around the age of eighteen the creases which will make him unhappy as well as preserving and perpetuating the social lie and the ancestral chains of the weak by the strong, have long hence been made on his brain: the spirit of authority, the famous sense of hierarchy, from whose yoke rather few individuals can escape. On the other hand, his material interests are already in play, which force him to be more and more passive with respect his masters, their laws, and their morality; they hold him there with increasing firmness, and never let him break free.

Finally, this is the age when he's about to fulfill his three years of obligatory military service. He will spend them in the most degrading promiscuity, along with ignorance, alcoholism, lubricity, even sadism, in fact, many of the vices created by authority. This is the final way people get bogged-down. By the end of this time, he'll be the submissive and vulgar being at whose side we dwell every day of our lives, and whose inertia and lack of understanding offend our desires for Beauty and Justice.

By this age, man is already perverse: libertarian education is a vaccine, but he has to be inoculated before the disease actually gets him.

By preserving him from the beginning of life from all the false beliefs kindled by the self-serving deceptions of the leaders and owners, from all adoration and demeaning respect, by teaching him contempt for all of Nature's coercive laws and rules and to despise anyone who bends in voluntary slavery, he will learn the path to dignity and joy.

While he's young, while he's still a child, he can be shown that a free man does not mistake dogmas for truths, that he sees natural reality powerfully and confidently, that he looks for causes and purposes in all phenomena, that he controls, debates all proclaimed opinions and principles, shatters the tyranny of prejudices, anti-natural moralities, and laws made for the benefit of certain classes, that, ultimately, he doesn't abjectly respect the institutions they've established in order to weaken any desire for emancipation by their slaves.

Instead of this, what do we currently see? How, in the schools where the lives of children and young men are prepared, is the highly esteemed bourgeois system of education and instruction put into practice?

Sadly, all the bourgeois teachers may well sing the praises of the school as they've made it, especially the primary schools, which aims primarily at the poor and ignorant classes, but they'll never be able to convince the sensible of any spectacular results, because the effects too plain which prove the opposite is the case.

Yes, education is more widespread in our day than under the *Ancien Régime* or even some thirty years ago. But what sort of an education is it, really?

An education which, as paradoxical as it might initially seem, neither aims at nor in fact produces free men, but only slaves.

Instead they are, as in the times of feudalism and monarchy, slaves who are physically attached to the lord's glebe, and docile subjects of the king, they're slaves who are economically and morally enslaved to society, to the State, these entities which are facades hiding the domineering and plundering minority. People no longer speak in the name of the King, but only in the name of Society, of the State. People no longer invoke divine right or feudal rights, but only legal rights, and these are no more the expression of the will of the majority of the nation, or even of elite individualities, than the "rights" of the *Ancien Régime* were in harmony with the desires and aspiration of the people. It's no longer the lords and priests who deprive the worker of the product of his labor, now it's the bosses, the capitalists, the proprietors, the speculators, the government officials, and a hundred other sorts of parasites.

The slaves are no longer called serfs, but citizens.

There are still priests charged with teaching the same lies, lawmakers, judges, police, and an army serving to defend property from attack by their impoverished victims and to guarantee power from aggression on the part of the enchained.

We know that if the title, not even the social but the governmental one, has changed, the merchandise handed down to the people remains the same, as odious as previously under deceitful appearances.

The official curriculum is created to perpetuate this state of affairs. An instrument of the classes where, reigning through money and position, these true masters of the Masses are found, it is organized and practiced in such a way that the solitary island remains such while thinking himself a free man.

In a preface to Tolstoy, Emile Bergerat wrote: "I'm one of those philosophers who think that the social question can be boiled down to a problem of education. It would be easy to see and predict the fate of a generation on basis of the pedagogical data of the education it has received."

Although seeming somewhat exclusive, this observation is quite apt. He's right: it's because of the education and instruction given to children, the young people, in the primary schools, the high schools and colleges, that society has become what it now is, prolonging the precarious existence which the stupidity, ignorance, and weakness of the masses give it, qualities cherished by the teachers who have often, in moments of sincerity, expressed regret at having granted their slaves an education that was too strong, and a love of liberty which was too great for their liking.

To this effect, the State implicitly cultivates two kinds of education: one for the children of the poor, the workers, that is, the Masses, — and one for the children of the wealthy classes.

In the primary schools, both secular and religious, children are taught that if a man is poor he should be content with his fate, or his God-given lot, depending on which school he's in, — following the prescriptions of the established morality, submitting to the laws, which are equal for all, naturally, — in other words, that he should obey whoever holds power or wealth and whoever condescends to prolong his life by giving him a job.

As a consolation prize, he's granted his liberty, so long as he obeys all the laws, — that he will only find fraternity in society, — and, above all, that he will be the equal of those in the highest positions: the greatest, the supreme flattery which tranquilizes all possible desire for rebellion by the good people: he is his master's equal, he has the same rights as him and the latter has identical duties to his own. I discern subtle and poignant realities which are there to steal his rights and leave his duties intact, while his master gets the opposite treatment. But he's been so perfectly stupefied from the earliest age that he'll die without ever realizing the truth.

The primary school is the school of resignation and weakness.

At religious schools they enslave in God's name, and in the secular ones, in the name of society. The same respect for the same dogmas, called by different names, is inculcated in both places. God and society command enjoin the same duties on the masses, which they must fulfill, under penalty, in the first case, of divine thunders and eternal punishment in Hell, and with the latter, the tortures of conscience. Besides which, to second the punishments which might seem uncertain in coming, the Law, as it is carefully pointed out, will be sure to make them comply with these so-called duties with the most vivid kinds of punishment.

In sum, in the primary schools, whether secular or religious, the children of the Masses are made into *good citizens* who are good at producing high profits for the capitalists and proprietors, to defend their property during a period of three years in forced labor with a regiment, or by death on the field of carnage, — *good citizens*, gentle ewes obedient to the shepherds who keep them sheared, patriots, voting *entirely* for one candidate of whatever shade who will beat on their drum to summon his cronies, and will take advantage of their naive confidence to make a good living, all the while renewing the laws which, in

the guise of reforms, make the social turpitude
perpetual.

In primary education, man is made into a creature
with neither willpower nor dignity. Unfit for the life
of the mind due his restricted intellect, knowing
nothing of real life, incapable of initiative, deprived of
profound and rational convictions, he is forever
subject to every exaction which his master's
selfishness might bring require of him.

This master will be the child who was raised in these
secular and religious high schools and colleges. From
the outset they're practical, for pecuniary reasons
which are obvious only to the children of the rich,
these establishments are nurseries for leaders and
property owners. These children and young men are
also hear talk about God and society, the respect
these abstractions deserve, the duties to be fulfilled,
about the Fatherland they must love and serve, but,
by means of the clever distinctions of philosophy and
political economy, they are then made to understand
that it's good for them to know about these things,
but it's less so for to take them seriously, and that
they are simply tools for governance.

So that, when they have become men of power and
wealth, they can do their part to impart them to the
People, in order to train the *good citizens* who will be
necessary for them, the bourgeoisie, to satisfy their
greed, vanity, lusts, laziness, and all the
concupiscence which might yet appear under the

twin influences of sloth and power, — if they pretend to believe, if they invoke them when it serves their purposes, nothing could be better. But they must not believe in them, like those weak liars who end up believing their own stories, lest they be crushed like mere proletarians.

This subtly hypocritical education, this two-faced morality which the Jesuits once secretly monopolized, is no longer the exclusive endowment of this confraternity. Although they're called secular, the State-establishment secondary teaching, the schools for the Republic's wealthy, educate the children of their bourgeois clientele in a spirit whose Jesuitism might make Loyola's disciples jealous!

In the schools for the poor, as well as in those for the rich, only one thing is taught in the same way: that society and all its institutions are held up by the sacred principle of Authority.

"Outside of her, no salvation" is said to both poor and rich alike. Thus, to each individual nursed on faith in this dogmatic principle, it then seems impossible to do anything socially and individually without the blessing of Authority. We have daily proofs of this before our eyes.

I said that Authority is taught equally, but through the differences in education indicated above, the children in the schools for the poor learn to endure this authority, while the children in the schools for the rich learn there how to use it — and abuse it.

Thus, from childhood up, at the school as well as in the family, man is tangled in the network of Authority. Whether rich or poor, without an extraordinary virility and a willingness to risk his life, he will be unable to get out of it, whether he is compelled to submit to it or compelled to make someone else submit to it, although naturally this second obligation is less of a nuisance than the first one.

The school is authoritarian in its results. It's also authoritarian in its organization. There, the child's educator is called his Master. The scholarly staff is classified into a hierarchy and the students are also classified in turn.

Among the students, the teachers select a few who are most given to malice, sneakiness, and submissiveness, and they assign them the role of "monitors". In this way they are trained to be snitches, corporals, and foremen. They're taught to love and respect the orders they receive. The slogan "divide and conquer" is as old as Authority itself; every good authoritarian system applies it to some extent, according to the wiliness of the leaders.

The teacher issues orders and the student must obey without attributing any reason to them but his the indisputable will. Discipline reigns. It's the regiment in miniature!

The subjects taught comprise many little dogmas, so to speak, so that, often, all the student has to do is memorize and retain them. It's pointless for him to reflect, think, and reason about the subjects taught; instead he should simply engrave the view of his Master in his memory, so that they can replace his own views. In this way, narrow brains, graced with prejudice, empty slogans, redundant phrases, and idiotic proverbs are formed. A pupil who disputes the teacher's views is a subversive, and is punished in various ways for such audacity, and he's set up to be tamed, subdued through persecution; he's humiliated, rendered hateful, hypocritical, and as colorless as his fellow students — unless the a rebellious spirit develops in him, that spirit which will keep him from getting bogged down, and will make a man of him despite the pedagogues.

On the other hand, the good fool, who's incapable of rationality but has a good memory, is an excellent student, and is both approved and rewarded.

Ultimately, and from school onwards, all possibility of initiative, all desire for investigation, all personal feelings are suppressed in man, that is, human individuality is crushed in the seed. Isn't Society there to give the individual his assigned role in existence? From then on he has no need to learn to act freely or examine anything for himself.

And so, through these mechanical teaching methods, any liberty which might potentially be in the child is annihilated. No less harmful is the carefully selected curriculum.

We've already seen what kind of Jesuitical morality is imparted to him. As an example, let's now take History, which forms part of the curriculum of secondary education. From the purely individual, as well as from the social perspective, this is a subject of the highest importance; its rational development might be extraordinarily fertile and lead to nearly immediate results.

But, for the teaching of this subject to add to that energetic impulse which must motivate the brains of today and of tomorrow towards an always nobler future, it must happen quite differently from how it is now taught. For, to avoid following the lead of Father Loriquet in very deed, it might nevertheless be placed under this saintly patronage in the sense that, if the materiality of facts is quite faithfully reported, what is deduced from them, — when conclusions are drawn at all, — in view of education, is, by the most basic logic, either mistaken or consciously falsified.

Already, the way of teaching history seems detestable to more than one sensible mind, in that it sets out from the dawn of times, from what's imprecise, which is explained in minute detail to the detriment of our contemporary era, which is, however, more interesting to us, since our lives are a related totality of recent events, and all the goings-on of the 19th century.

The objection might be raised that the French history textbooks used in the schools relate events which occurred in this century up to around 1889. That's true, but in oral development, — whether due to a poor distribution of programs, or rather the bias of professors in not revealing to their students the mystery which for them surrounds the age of the revolutions of 1830 and of 1848, the coup d'état of Louis-Napoléon, the Commune and the republican, socialist and anarchist movement of the last thirty years, — they stop at the advent of Charles X, when, however, nobody stops at the fall of the First Empire. At any rate, the facts about revolutions are generally passed over, along with anything that might help to educate the mind of a free human, on pretext of not being "political"!

Likewise, when the professor deals with the middle ages and the times called "modern", he doesn't draw out the implications of the Jacqueries, the Commune movement, the rebellions in Flanders, the Reform, the intellectual agitation of the Encyclopedists, or even the Revolution.

But, what should be told, both to children and young men, in every school, without distinction, is the whole truth and it should come with a commentary pointing at Liberty. And, above all, in the schools patronized by the children of the workers, the proletariat, it would be necessary to portray for the mind of the Masses, while they're children, their own history, the history of their class in some way, which is much more important to it from the perspective of its emancipation than the anecdotic side of history, the stories of battles, the dates of wars and treaties and such secondary matters on which the memory is overworked while thought is neglected.

But it would be indispensable to this end that the professors should not be the servants, either of the State or any kind of leader, ministers for the worship of ignorance, this capital available to every exploiter.

What would be necessary, for example, would be to stop kindling amazement in the young man at the displays of grandeur of Louis XIV, but to teach him that this so-called glory came at the cost of much suffering by the masses.

It would be to stop saying that Louis XV, a frivolous monarch, reacted to generalized discontent by saying: "Screw the future", but rather to show them the true role of a master, whatever title he bears, whatever "right" he claims, and show the repercussions for others of his selfishness and his will, which were based on unlimited liberty for himself and the subjection of all.

It would be to stop simply mentioning that Louis XVI died, but to explain that he was executed on 21 January 1793 as the symbol of monarchical tyranny and all "divine right", rather than as a simple human being.

It would include ceasing to teach the worship of murder on the fallacious pretext of patriotism, singing the praises of Napoleon, but rather to communicate the horror which should arise in every sound mind at the tale of the reign of this imperial director of massacres, and inspire them with a contempt for war.

Along with so many other things of an interest which has priority over all other considerations, which are, besides, usually hypocritical!

Ultimately, teaching the People's History should, on every occasion, be to proceed to the awakening of the People's thought about what it once was, what it is, and what it might be. If this didn't pave the way for a definitive revolution, if this word terrifies the ruling class, it would at least constitute the evolution of men towards a milieu of liberty, and therefore, of natural justice.

But the ways of guiding mankind are always the same, from ancient times up to the present. It's always, on one side, the same lie inculcated in the poor, the enslaved, and on the other, the same profusion of truth joined to the same spirit of duplicity, spread among the rich and the rulers. This is how societies based on the exploitation of weakness by strength, of ignorance by wiliness, are created and preserved.

History itself, true history, is clear and precise on this point. The further one looks into the past, the more one finds means which might differ on points of detail, but not in principles.

And we freethinkers have no interest in making *good citizens*, but instead many *individuals*, and if authoritarian education, in its aims and its means, interest us at all, it's only to criticize and destroy it, and we'll bring all our passion and rationality together, in a single will of complete liberty, to make that happen.

II.

Two men, two honorable educationists have, each in their own way, made efforts to bring liberty to education — and to life through education.

They are: Leo Tolstoy and Paul Robin.

Studying the theory and practice of their systems will guide us, whether by trimming back or assimilation, to an understanding of the tools useful in the service of a libertarian education[9].

Tolstoy is the creator of a pedagogical system through liberty, which he has professed and applied since 1862. It's in the Russian province of Tula, at Yasnaya Polyana, a village of around 600 inhabitants, where he has applied his theory in practice. There he has

---

[9] Having tried, in the second part of *l'Education et la Liberté*, to give a synthetic overview of the pedagogical systems of Tolstoy and Robin, I've tried to take the necessary information from the documents which these two innovators have placed at the public's disposal. For Tolstoy, this information has been borrowed from *The School of Yasnaya Polyana. Le Rapport du Cercle d'Etudes sociales de Paris*, 1870 (P. Robin, recorder), has furnished me with these two relating to Robin. Here, one will find, sometimes at length, sometimes in brief, the words of Tolstoy and Robin themselves.

organized a school of a kind that's free of cost and free in its nature, which he leads in person, with the help of two teachers, and which some fifty children attend, both girls and boys.

Let's watch it in action.

Already, outside the school, the student is absolutely free. Unlike other places he doesn't have this material burden of books and notebooks, and the no less heavy intellectual burden of lessons and homework which prolong the student's day into the family time, turning study into torture.

In the school the child is also free, even to do nothing. Emile Bergerat informs us that "There, the master[10] plays no other role than that of a living dictionary, accessible to all, which each curiosity consults or even neglects, according to their temperament, whim, or wishes." The master, to use the consecrated term, here is no master in the true sense of the term: in no way does he have the powers he might take for granted elsewhere.

According to Tolstoy, the teacher should only aim at offering, subject to the student's choice, the known tools, and to know which ones would facilitate his studies and sweeten the learning process through the freedom of choice.

---

[10] (Translator): I.e. teacher.

From this freedom, relations are created and established between pupil and master where sincerity, simplicity, and confidence reign together, magnificently. The master becomes something like a benevolent father or an experienced brother to the child, and gets him to share what he learns joyfully.

This shows that none of the violence coming from a contempt for the human personality takes place at Yasnaya Polyana. There, not only the futility, but also the harm in such things has been recognized. Non-corporal punishments are also off limits. "Our group of children, who are simple, open creatures, must remain pure from this lie, from this criminal belief in the legitimacy of punishment, from which it would follow that vengeance is right as long as we call it punishment."

Consequently, rewards are also absent. An unheard-of idea in our schools, and a shock, is the fact that the only rewards the students receive are in morale, in their satisfaction of their desires for knowledge, desires which Tolstoy stimulates when he makes learning attractive by freedom. Having reached a certain age, the students of this school become animated by such a passion for learning that they get annoyed when younger children interrupt their work.

The great argument of the authoritarian educationists against the liberty of the school is the same one used by authoritarian sociologists against liberty in society. Liberty, they also say, brings "disorder".

As to what concerns the school, in the views of Tolstoy, who speaks after experimentation, what they call disorder, is only disorder on the outside: it is actually order in reality, since it is natural; this disorder is thus a useful, and even indispensable, form of children's activity, as strange and annoying as it may at first seem to the teacher.

This "disorder, or order in freedom" also seems so terrifying because we've been educated by the authoritarian system and so it's hard for us to conceive its opposite, as, for identical reasons, it's nearly impossible for a contemporary man to think, *ex abrupto,* of the idea of anarchy and the social milieu which might result from its practical application.

Tolstoy has observed that, if the disorder gets worse and worse, knowing no limits, to the point that you begin to fear that only brute force can stop it, all you have to do is wait a little to see this disorder, or this energy, appeasing itself and producing a much better and more stable order than anything that compulsion might put in its place.

As a complement of the abrogation of punishment and reward, class rankings, which Tolstoy still used in the first years of the creation of his school, had been definitively done away with.

Moreover, this custom fell into disuse of its own accord: after a few years under the rule of liberty, the students began to realize their true worth and were able to judge their own work and base their subsequent efforts on their personal evaluation.

Plenty of other new means for the transmission of knowledge, grounded in liberty and coming from experience and logical deduction, have been brought by Tolstoy into the workings of his school. As he says, he's reaped nothing but success with respect to the sum of knowledge acquired by the students and the extension of their intellectual and moral faculties.

Thus, making use of a method of transmission by liberty, Tolstoy forms well instructed men, who are acquainted with a certain kind of liberty. But this liberty — a partial one, as we'll see — is not full liberty.

If Tolstoy advises the use of liberty in the school as a means of transmitting knowledge, he continues like other places to impart false beliefs to the child, to train him up, above all, in the perverting religions of deism and patriotism.

In these peculiar educational circumstances there is a flagrant and deplorable contradiction, which, later on, leads to a fatal confusion in how they think and live.

They might become good at avoiding the direct coercion of the representatives of authority or the surrounding social environment, as asserted by certain moral customs or laws which they refuse and reject, but what they do become good at is suffering indirect coercion, coercion by persuasion, which constitutes the greatest power of governance held by the rulers and proprietors.

The Doukhobors, a little Russian population of the Caucasus region, of whom Tolstoy has said so much in recent years, present a striking example of this dangerous moral situation.

The Doukhobors refuse all military service to the Czar, but they believe in God and practice Christianity. Their religion deprives them of any the benefit from this anti-militarist attitude, since their strict adherence to Christ's teaching "Thou shalt not kill", means they have to go willingly to prison or be massacred rather than kill the Cossacks who are sent to conscript them by force.

Those educated by Tolstoy are condemned to similar contradictory attitudes.

The reason is because at the school of Yasnaya Polyana, the only thing that's good, the only thing which is libertarian, the only thing which develops the individuality, is the method of transmission of knowledge, while the bad part, since it's authoritarian and leads to slavery, is the subject matter taught as part of the secondary education of the individual, such as history, morality, philosophy, etc., which are taught according to an anti-scientific spirit.

To go against Science is to hamper all truth and reason.

Thus, Tolstoy combats materialism and atheism, as a spiritualist and a deist. And if he seems anti-militarist, he remains — what an antithesis — a patriot! His teaching is therefore both religious and nationalistic. In the *School of Yasnaya Polyana*, a book in which he explains his system of pedagogy, he himself says[11] that by Russian history he seeks to awaken "national feeling" in the heart of the child. And he says that he knows no better reading material for the children and even the common people than the Bible.

> I repeat my conviction, which has been deduced from experience alone, that without the Bible in our society, the development of children and adults is impossible. The Bible is the only book for early and childhood reading. The Bible, in form and foundation, should serve as a model for all children's texts and reading books. A popular edition of the Bible would be the best book for the people[12].

---

[11] (Translator): See Tolstoy, *Yasnaya Polyana School*, chapter 32, "Russian History".
[12] (Translator): Ibid. chapter 31, "The Bible for Children".

But the Bible is a poetically ornamented tissue of inanity, ridiculous lies, and common errors which Science has long ago disproved.

Aside from discipline, the school of Yasnaya Polyana therefore has nothing on our ignoramus schools.

Without, for all that, showing the least sectarianism, we can consequently say that using the tools of liberty to transmit the errors and lies of deism and nationalism, contrary to science and reason, is not exactly doing the work of emancipation.

This is why, for my part, approving the method of transmission, but criticizing the nature of the subjects taught, — which is the essential thing, — I cannot share the enthusiasm of some for Tolstoy's educational system. I find more snobbery and misunderstanding in such enthusiasm than well-reasoned admiration.

Paul Robin was able to avoid this huge failing in Tolstoy's system. With him we attain a manifestly superior level of achievement to the one just discussed.

Robin's system might have realized the libertarian pedagogical ideal if it had subordinated the activity of the Individual less to the Collectivity. For, in the spirit of Robin, education is only given to the individual to make a social functionary of him.

He defines the role of the individual in Society and that of education in the life of the Individual like this:

> Man is at once an isolated being, an incomplete whole, and an organ of the collectivity. Considered from the first point of view, he is a consumer, he has rights; in the second he is a producer, he has duties.
>
> At first he is incapable of producing, and only consumes: at this point he only has rights, the right to physical and intellectual development.
>
> But, a little later on, man begins to have duties to fulfill; the possibility of production appears and begins to increase. At this moment, the organ of the collectivity should swing into action in order to make him capable of fulfilling, as soon as possible, a determinate function in the world, or even better, a certain number of functions.
>
> Integral instruction aims at relating men to the perfection in these two perspectives.

The spirit which presided over education in Robin's system was therefore authoritarian, — not, perhaps, as brutishly and ferociously as with the bourgeois, but authoritarian still.

The means of transmission were themselves largely authoritarian. However, a relative level of familiarity was allowed between teachers and pupils. Efforts were made to stimulate the curiosity of the young man instead of dogmatically imprinting knowledge on his brain. The control of student meetings, with or without the teacher, was handed over to the students.

Emulation was organized in an entirely different way from that used elsewhere and much more sensibly. Recognizing that class ranking is never an expression of justice (since it consists in an illogical comparison between people differing in age, temperament, and ability), Robin thought it dreadful: the child already has a feeling of justice in himself; class ranking, which is always unjust, as we have seen, withers this feeling in him and creates jealousy and hatred. And so he got rid of class rankings and replaced them with a personal kind of emulation, by comparing the student's present with his previous work. No parallel was made between himself and his classmates. This mode of emulation gave the student a real idea of his progress or shortcomings and he inspired him to believe in science while sparing him the sterilizing inferiority resulting from jealousy.

Rational, the system of education of Robin could do nothing better to proclaim his desire to advance towards the total emancipation of humanity than by setting up as a pedagogical principle and as a practice, the coeducation of the sexes.

If we consider that the task of education in the family usually falls to the woman, we'll realize the immense utility of educating future mothers.

Only coeducation of the sexes can grant women the liberty which would come from the equality of the sexes, when it's finally gained.

The movement called feminist can never bring this result by itself. From this point of view, it has limited importance, having so far incarnated more of a petty idea of the struggle of women and men, of the feminine creature against the masculine, than of the rebellion of women against the Society which enslaved her along with her male counterpart, an idea, ultimately, of the complete liberation which men in search of justice wish for all of humanity without distinction of sex.

Aside from the fact that women are mothers and undertake most of the children's education in the family, they are also spouses, i.e. the companions of men. And so it's only logical for men and women, who have to live together in Society, to become more familiar with each other by living, studying, and working together throughout their youth.

One problem seems to arise: that of immortality which might result when children, young people of different sexes, spend time together.

Robin foresaw this objection and only his bad-faith opponents, the clerical and nationalistic slanderers, could criticize him for having favored immorality in the orphanage of Cempuis, where he tried his system.

It is possible that, when such a system is finding its feet, especially if its students are the children of present-day society, premature desires might arise in the minds of the students. Preventative measures, non-corporeal but moral, are necessary, but gradually they become useless as knowledge of natural truths replaces ignorance and mystery in the students' minds, and by the educators' knowledge of the needs and aptitudes of the young.

Besides, since this immorality can't be blamed on Nature, but rather the corruption of our badly organized Society and the irrational and anti-natural system used in present-day schools, which Robin rightly called "barracks-seminaries", the possibility for its occurrence will vanish as the coeducation of the sexes occurs in the midst of a society based on reason.

It's by hiding nothing from the young man and the young girl, as opposed to what authoritarian educators do, by facilitating understanding, to keep them from suffer the realities which differentiate them and the natural laws blindly, by teaching about the sexual functions (an education which should be given no more or less importance than the other branches of human activity), that we can do away with the unhealthy state of the brains of children who have reached the age of puberty. In this way, too, we can get rid of the moral and intellectual gap between men and women which now exists, and which is deliberately enlarged by the partisans of masculine preponderance, a difference which puts women in a state of inferiority vis-a-vis men, who become their enemies and tyrants.

We can begin to destroy this false modesty and false sentimentality which create so many physical and moral problems during the lives of the individuals who distorted in this way.

Every opportunity is given to the young man, before the conventional age of majority or marriage, to know these realities. The hypocrisy of Society and the world refuses it to the young girl, who is brought to marriageable age in complete ignorance of the natural obligations of her sex and is therefore vulnerable to the demands and diseases of her husband.

A full knowledge of Nature, imparted gradually in the coeducation of the sexes, to all women, nips these monstrosities the bud, which exist in present-day life.

Let nobody say, as normal as it is, that such an education destroys all love of beauty and life. Nobody thinks that the subjection of woman to her husband, that the prostitution to which he can deliver her without great danger for himself, that the syphilis which he might give her instead of a dowry, that the sadism, the sickly lustiness, and the brutality to which he can give free reign at her expense, that the theft of her possession authorized by the law, that all these and other calamities also constitute a love of life's beauty for the feminine being.

Besides, for everyone who has previously been taught to love and understand Nature, what might nowadays be called the mysteries of generation can only seem noble and grand.

Ultimately, Robin did not keep, on the religious question, to the kind of somewhat benevolent neutrality professed by the secular educators with regard to the lie and its supports. He taught atheism. He taught what every man of good sense knows today; that is: that God is a myth created by the first intelligent authoritarians to establish their rule, and that the ministers of this imaginary being are clever parasites who exploit ignorance. In this way he cast from the human brain the phantom of God, and replaced it with veridical and vivifying Science.

As for patriotism, he annihilated it by a firmly taught internationalism. He knew that the lie of the Fatherland was invented for reasons similar to those which led men to dream up a God, and by individuals of the same stripe. He prepared men for the fertile and blessed fraternity of peoples, for the realization of the terrestrial Republic.

What abominable crimes! The coalition of mystifiers hasn't forgiven him and he's still atoning for it with his misfortune.

I've said that Robin's system may leave too much space for authoritarianism, albeit rather little by comparison with bourgeois education, — but, all things considered, we must recognize that, given the age in which it was thought up, the plan for this system represented what might be considered the most sensible and the nearest to the ideal of libertarian pedagogy.

However that may be, Robin's system remains the one which the final society will put to use on a basis of authority, Collectivism, the unavoidable transitory state of the future, which must precede the libertarian milieu of the future.

It's well known that Robin, a man of powerful will, did try out his system in the orphanage of Cempuis, but the coalition of clerics and nationalists, these supports for Dogma, managed get this irreconcilable enemy of lies dismissed from his post, and modify the spirit of his school which, now, is hardly different from other teaching establishments.

Every attempt to regenerate the Individual through education has ended in a conception superior to those of Tolstoy and Robin, in the sense that it takes what is good and libertarian in each of them and leaves behind what is bad, authoritarian.

From Tolstoy's system it got the means of transmission, the libertarian method of education and instruction, — and from the Robin's system its subject matter, its grounding in science, truth, and logic, — in addition, it is equipped with its own characteristics, which are inherent in the anarchic idea.

This is the conception of the Libertarian School, which was trialed nearly three years ago in Paris among a handful of freethinkers.

The Libertarian Schools must rise and grow, as a peaceful threat to the skills of official education, both secular and religious, and carry on, in a wider sense, the incomplete labor of its precursors.

It should educate free men instead of molding social slaves, making autonomous individuals instead of molding *citizens*.

Sheltered from the official curriculum, from all authoritarian intrusion, the initiators of this free school should have taught men to guide themselves through life, to develop their own initiative, to consult only their own conscience, to expect no rewards for their acts aside from their own satisfaction.

Discipline, violence, class rankings, punishment and reward, as well as dogmatic education, had been excluded from this school.

But, for lack of financial backing, this free institution has limited its teaching to basic evening courses, after which it succumbed definitively.

Nevertheless, it left a milestone further along the route of evolution.

Certain sociologists predict that a social alteration will happen under the influence of economic conditions. This is true, but should it not also be, in a less equal proportion, the work of education? In my opinion, it will not be stable unless it has this dual origin.

Evolution must precede revolution, which is its logical consequence, its sanction.

Of all the revolutions that we've seen carried out, none has had any truly emancipatory outcome; when they're consummated, those who made them and their descendants have always returned to the same old mistakes, their slavery only changed its form. The revolutions were fruitless because the individuals concerned had not completed their evolution.

Man always wants to promote what he thinks best. His egoism, which is, essentially, only an individual expression of the species' instinct for self-preservation, encourages this. But if he has no sense for what is better and what is best, what can he do but stagnate?

It's precisely because his egoism has been poorly educated that it doesn't turn sooner towards Liberty, the fruitful wellspring of happiness. He can't see that, as far as social organization is concerned, something other than what we now have might offer better chances for him to prosper. He's in pain, but he doesn't know how to cure his disease. Educate him seriously, broadly, open his eyes to all truth, to all information, and his activity will focus on Liberty.

But, let's never stop repeating, it's crucial for this education to start in childhood, in this way leaving no room for the authoritarian spirit.

It's through libertarian education that we'll be able to make individuals — both men and women — who are intelligent, good, strong and just, free men, who will be able to make the Society of free Justice.

CANNON FODDER

1913

In 1904, at the au national congress of Bourges, organized by the General Confederation of Labor, the delegate of the Bourse du Travail of Saint-Denis and of the Fédération Syndicale of the Miners of Pas-de-Calais encouraged a "womb strike" as a means of immediate amelioration of the fate of the proletarians, and as a revolutionary permanent means with an eye to their complete emancipation. And he ended by saying: "You'll see, comrades, panic in the military and capitalist castes at the decreased birth rate!"

The moment for the panic has come, at least for the more clear-sighted bourgeois, who are the most careful about their class's interests. Without making minor political distinctions of right and left, in the dailies we see a symphony of lamentations: "The country is in danger!" which might be translated as: "The profits of our capitalists are compromised!"

And for the love of God — i.e., the Fatherland — they tell the proletarians: "Make more children for us so that we can have soldiers."

The craziest and most repugnant plans are encouraged to combat the "scourge" of a supposed "depopulation". A first extra-parliamentary commission on depopulation having aborted, which is a smooth irony, a second commission has been convoked by the government in order to seek the most effective means for getting the individuals of the French collectivity to breed like rabbits. Naturally, this assembly is exclusively chosen from the bourgeoisie, the proletarians having no voice in the matter, and is composed of men, since women are considered as a layer of eggs whom the male, as and when he likes, makes or doesn't make children, but whom he should impregnate anyways at least four times with ultimate success if he wants to duly called a good citizen. More fortunate than its predecessor, this commission might yet give birth... to a mouse. It hardly matters. What we need to remember is that it is essentially a coercive institution of one class and one sex.

Let's observe in passing that the bourgeoisie, from the good apostles campaigning for "repopulation" to even the most obscure capitalists, in pursuit of the usual hypocrisy which remains a privilege of theirs, never act by the slogans of their own patriotism, since, when they do reproduce, they tend to limit how many children they have: the man, in his desire to preserve and intensify his means of struggle and enjoyment; the woman, to more fully enjoy her life and avoid the pains involved in procreation.

Although this is a well-known fact, the proofs bear repeated publication.

Here, to this point, are some meaningful statistics, worked out by comrade Ernest Cordonnier, for the year 1901, according to the *Weekly Bulletin of Municipal Statistics of the City of Paris*, for three wealthy districts and three poor ones.

District #	**7th**	**8th**	**16th**	**11th**	**19th**	**20th**
Live births	1,468	1,230	1,795	5,636	3,779	4,471
Stillborn	65	56	101	413	258	306
Total births	1,533	1,283	1,896	6,049	4,037	4,776
Total population	98,500	102,625	117,087	233,699	143,187	163,601
Birth rate per 10,000 couples	311	250	323	517	564	584

Bourgeois districts   Proletarian districts

"It's easy to see," comrade Cordonnier adds, "that the lowest birth rate is in the 5th district (250) and that the highest is that of the 20th (584), which leads to the truly striking conclusion that, while 100 bourgeois children are born in the 8th, 233 poor are born in the 20th[13]."

This statistic is corroborated by what a notorious Anti-Malthusian, Mr. Charles Richet, professor in the Faculty of Medicine at Paris, produced in a study on *L'Accroissement de la population francaise*[14]. Mr. Richet categorized births by Parisian quarters, per 1,000 inhabitants:

Six quarters with maximal birth rate		Six quarters with minimal birth rate	
Père Lachaise	39.1	St-Thomas-d'Aquin	14.4
Pont-de-Flandre	36.7	Chaussée-d'Antin	14.4
Gares d'Orléans	35.3	Place Vendôme	14.0
Javel	32.7	Invalides	13.7
Maison-Blanche	32.7	Madeleine	12.9

---

[13] *Régénération*, August 1905.

[14] Revue scientifique, 25 April 1891. The statistic has been reproduced by *Régénération*, Nov. 1905.

La Chapelle   32.   Porte-Dauphine   10.3
                               7

Average per 1,000 inhabitants

Quarters (rich) with minimal birth rate   13.3

Quarters (poor) with maximal birth rate   34.9

Here is another related statistic on Parisian birth rates, published by Mr. Clementel, in his Report on the war budget for 1911, given in the name of the Commission of the Chamber of deputies[15]:

For every 1,000 married women from 15 to 50 years old, there are:

108   births in the very poor quarters

99   ” ” ” poor ”

72   ” ” ” comfortable ”

65   ” ” ” quite comfortable ”

53   ” ” ” rich ”

34   ” ” ” very rich ”

---

[15] According to the *Temps*, 3 Feb. 1911.

A particularly suggestive document is the "Inquest on the ruling classes and repopulation", carried out by the *Intransigeant*[16]. The average given was 1 ¼ children per bourgeois couple. Since the conclusion from this study, which was in fact undertaken in an anti-Malthusian spirit, was too clear and too subversive, *someone* intervened and it was quickly withdrawn.

— The rabbit-hutch for the proletarians, sure, but as for ourselves, the bourgeoisie, we'll avoid such a horror!

The bourgeois are right to limit their births, since they get its benefit. In a different way of thinking, they are even right to want their subjects to breed like rabbits, since this creates numerous slaves for them. But, as in other circumstances of life, the latter are wrong to follow the Jesuitical precepts of their masters — their enemies, if we believe the fabulist on the matter.

***

And so, the birth rate has dropped in France, — along with most of the old countries of Europe, especially Germany. Up to and including 1906, there was only a tendency to what is habitually called "depopulation" and which can, for some time now, only be called a *de-overpopulation*. The year 1907 inaugurated true

---

[16] *L'Intransigeant*, 2, 3, 5, 10, 15, 19, and 28 August 1908.

de-overpopulation: according to the official statistics, the birth rate lags behind the rate of deaths to the tune of 19,920. After many years of minor excesses in the birth rate, the deficit came in 1911, the last known annual census, of 34,869, — a fortunate trend, but not enough to satisfy us.

Given that the bourgeois are alarmed at this false depopulation, they should logically, talk to us about repopulation, which, in reality, would end up aggravating the overpopulation which is our present reality. This is what they do, but it's clear how much of a failure that is for them!

A single argument is invoked by them to support their thesis. It is of a patriotic order: on the day of a great international slaughter, the French capitalists won't have enough cannon fodder at their disposal to defend their property. And on that day, as we know, they'll need plenty.

In 1903, senator Piot wrote to Mr. Combes, the president of the Conseil des ministres, to point out that the contingent conscripted in November of the same year was 34,000 men smaller than in the previous year. He said:

> In a single blow, the army of the Republic would lose three divisions: a deficit all the more regrettable from the point of view of national security since the headcount of the contingent of the German army register, instead, an increase of 15,000 men versus its predecessor... The peril is

> pressing!... The public powers are charged with the grandeur of the Republic. It's up to them to show that true patriotism consists in resolutely foreseeing the day when our army, consequent to the crisis of depopulation which I never tire of pointing out and whose progress must be halted at any cost, would no longer contain the number of soldiers necessary for the national defense.

I cite this letter, which once made the rounds in the French press, because it is characteristic of the spirit which animates the rulers on the subject of population. But simply read the complaints of the lesser and greater supporters of the bourgeoisie in the papers; from the whitest Monarchists to the reddest republicans, they shamelessly confess that their fears are restricted to this one object: cannon fodder.

Where, then, does this agreement come from, of men who seem to be political enemies? It's because politics is nothing if it's not the art of *cooking* the *pears*[17]. Arguments arise as to the proper manner of preparing the dish: should it be the royalist, the Bonapartist, or the republican sauce? But as regards the need to eat them, all discussion ends. Everyone shares the same view: they will be eaten.

On vital questions, they quickly find agreement, provided they have interests in common, and that they know how to realize and manage them. All of the

---

[17] (Translator): French poire, i.e. sucker, chump.

bourgeois, whether their cap is white, black, or red, have an interest in common which they are aware of and pursue: they have an interest in the defense of their country against the capitalists of other countries.

Because the bourgeoisie, the capitalists, have a country, and only they have one: a patriotic proletarian is an idiot, for he has no country of his own, unless it's in the Valais...

A country is a syndicate of capitalists.

*
**

The existing relationship between population and war can't be usefully and frankly discussed without situating it in the terrain of class struggle. For, present society seems very much divided into two classes, whose interests are profoundly opposed: masters and slaves, rich and poor, bourgeoisie and proletariat, parasitic capitalists and the workers, manual or intellectual, creators of wealth.

It may be that a great number of individuals of the second class fail to see their own interests in full: but they still exist, and they're identical to those of the proletarian class as a whole, with which they are mixed.

That's the hard task: to make the proletarians, whose mentality is saturated with religiosity, understand that one must act in one's personal interest, just like one's boss does. It seems simple and the observer who is, while not completely superficial, still fails to get to the bottom of things, will object that no individual, in nature, is motivated by anything but self-interest. Sure, in principle; but the religious conception of life which the priest imparted to the proletarians keeps him, most often, from grasping his true interests and leads him to sacrifice himself to an interest opposite his own, as it becomes necessary to show him.

— What, our heckler will say, the individual, of the proletariat, is stupid enough not to know his own interests? And you, someone else, are going to point it out to him?

— Be sure of this: he's generally stupid enough not to see where his interest lies. And we who have been able to define it, may be able to let this ignorant man know that for him there are *fictive interests* and *real interests*. For example, for a proletarian with no country, fulfillment of the so-called duties which the priests of the patriotic religion teach him is the result of the false belief in the reality of an interest which is only fictive.

The idea of national solidarity, which in times of peace and war should unite all the individuals contained within certain boundaries called borders and established by the leaders of various countries, — this idea is a lie for the proletarians, because they have no real interest in national integrity, in which the bourgeois, themselves, have an interest, and because no solidarity links them to the latter, for there can be no solidarity except between individuals having interests in common.

The individual, man, is the only existent reality, by relation to these entities which a reasoning which is still imbued with metaphysics brings against him: Society, State, Country, etc.

Society is only an abstraction expressing the fact of the association of individuals. Yet, when the master feel the need, they invoke, as justification for their selfish acts, the interests of Society[18], the health of which they look out for, — all the more jealously since they are Society, the slaves being their things, thanks to the property of capital they hold, thanks to their strength, — a strength made of the ignorance and religiosity of these slaves.

Considering *their* society by relation to the other societies which divide the Earth among themselves and which are constituted according to authoritarian statues which differ slightly in form, but are identical in their aims: the exploitation of the slaves by the masters, — the capitalists call it: fatherland.

---

[18] By capitalizing the articles and nouns, I mean to express the holiness of things, according to the spirit of the mystical or positive religions.

For reasons of a purely economic order, disputes and quarrels do arise between the shepherds of these different herds, between the capitalists of these diverse countries, quarrels which the slaves stupidly rush to join. These disagreements are resolved with cannonballs. To withstand the blast and return it, fodder is required for the cannons, and the capitalist syndicates think, quite rightly, that the syndicate which has the best chance of winning is the one with the greatest force of resistance, the most human fodder to sacrifice in this shootout.

Consequently, they ask the proletarians to make children for them, men, for the "national defense", more precisely, for war, for (even though that is indifferent to us) we know that none of the belligerent nations ever attacks the other and that each only ever defends itself...

And so, for the edification of all future victims, and even previous victims, let's take a peek at the real causes of these wars.

*
**

Indeed! It's always for "noble" causes that the "brave" go to die!

The masters who declare the wars can give them an idealistic pretext: in reality, they have — it may be said: always — a cause or a motive of an economic order, which won't keep superficial minds from seeing an honorable cause in them every time, an ideal end.

The rulers will never be naive enough to openly state that in this, as in all they do, they obey a selfish motive and pursue economic ends. They have too hypocritically depreciated — for the others — selfish and material preoccupations, of their own, to talk this way. They will exploit the religious views which they promote in their subjects' minds; depending on circumstances, war will be waged for God, — the country's God, — for the Fatherland, for Civilization, for Progress, for Humanity...

It's time to see that with a more realistic eye.

Frédéric Passy says that:

> A man, who, for more than thirty years, has composed the treaties concluded by France, d'Hauterive, the chef de service at the Ministry of Foreign Affairs, has said — and rightly so — that nearly all wars, by whatever name they were called, were only wars of commerce, conquest, or depredation[19].

And Urbain Gohier says:

> War has been waged in Tunisia for the good Tunisian shippers, just as war has been waged in Tonkin for the customers of Jules Ferry, war came

---

[19] Frédéric Passy, *Les Causes économiques des guerres*.

to Dahomey for three Marseille businessmen and expeditions reached Guinea for the customers of the minister Delcassé; for the society Suberbie and Co., war is waged in Madagascar[20].

There, the deprived interests seem clear enough — after the fact — but, when the conquest of these territories was undertaken, it was to promote an idea, no doubt about it! I was quite young when the expedition of Dahomey took place, but I perfectly remember that a humanitarian ambition presided over it! Besides, the patriotic argument may be invoked alongside an argument for "justice". The rulers gladly proclaim that they are starting this or that war for the sake of the national honor in the person of a "compatriot" whose rights have been violated. And thus the cannon fodder is mobilized to "avenge" some capitalistic scoundrel whose excesses have provoked the legitimate rebellion of a population: this is the desired pretext for the dominance by armed force over a country that had been coveted.

Would the Turko-Balkan war, with its perks, such as the calculated assistance of this or that nation by this or that other, have been anything other than the violent dénouement of an imbroglio of economic interests? However, the ideal pretext was not lacking there. It was soon forgotten, the argument invoked by the allies to "come to the assistance of our enslaved brothers", of "delivering our Christian brothers from

---

[20] Urbain Gohier, *Sur la Guerre*.

the Muslim yoke": a snare, an illusion for the masses! In the end, the States allied with the Balkans annexed nearly all of the European part of Turkey.

Perhaps never better than on the occasion of the Austro-Serbian conflict, which was the outcome of the Turko-Balkan war, has the real motive of all war been manifest: in species, a necessity for the Serbian exports of a port on the Adriatic sea and a railway from the Danube to the Adriatic, in order, for Serbia, to escape its economic dependence on Austria-Hungary, — a port which is not, moreover, guaranteed, any more than the railway is, whose establishment has always been eluded by Turkey, as far as it was concerned, of connivance with Austria-Hungary. It may seem that, at these results the least of the Serbian proletarians might have an interest; but then the Austro-Hungarian proletarians would, on the other hand, have an interest in keeping these results from coming about, no matter what benefit, from a war, might fall to a nation, — by the effect of overpopulation and the play of social institutions, the proletarian remains a proletarian. For behind these enterprises, these conflicts, these supposedly national wars, the great capitalistic interests are watching, the interests of the rulers-owners unified nationally, who, for their part, find satisfaction there, because they're the strongest of all, — artificially, at any rate.

And here is the nature of the "arguments" for which, foolishly, patriotically, the proletarians of each of the Balkan countries, including Turkey, have consented to kill each other and for which the survivors will consent to giving birth to even more cannon fodder!

*
**

Economic war, — to use something like a pleonasm, — war can appear in two guises: it occurs, either between nations called civilized and peoples called inferior, or simply between nations called civilized.

The second case is often the consequence of the first one. The dispute generally originates in the desire for colonial conquest, which also drives two or more States who covet the same land.

An example from the past: the threat of war between Germany and France over Morocco. The dispute is, moreover, resolved as if a war took place: the German government consented to the invasion of the Moroccan territory by the French, but in exchange it asked for the gift of a part of the Congo. The French rulers, fearing defeat and insurrection, rushed to grant to their competitors whatever they wanted. The numerical weakness of a population in relation to another and the revolutionary spirit of this population are often, for the rulers, the beginnings of wisdom.

Another example from the past: the war between Italy and Turkey, disputing the possession of Tripolitania.

If, now, it's asked who and what the colonial conquests benefit, one quickly sees that they are always done to advance the interests of the ruling and possessing class and that they serve it for various ends.

Nobody is unware that overpopulation, that is, an excessive population relative to subsistence available in a country, profits the capitalists of this country in that it procures low-cost manpower for them, — among other things, the least of which is cannon fodder. But it's also important for this overpopulation not to exceed a decent limit: by their colonies, the capitalists, in this case, procure an outlet for an excessive part of the population.

Still, the possession of colonies for purposes of emigration, and also in the aim of extracting subsistence at some point, is not the only way to combat the outcomes of excessive overpopulation. Industrial and commercial expansion is another one, but this brings ills identical to those of colonialism, while multiplying the opportunities for international conflicts. At most, this tool also requires the existence of colonies at a certain point, no longer only to serve as receptacles for the surplus population and as a granary for surpluses, but also to extract the primary materials necessary for industry and to get the latter producing.

How, indeed, does a population manage to live — badly, of course — who, having extracted the utmost from its land by way of agricultural products, finds itself more numerous than the products of the earth will allow? It must now intensify the transformation of primary materials into manufactured objects and trade these objects, operations which lead to the theft of profit, which will serve for the acquisition of the missing foodstuffs. And can this be poured out more favorably than those offered by their colonies, of which, through customs legislation, the metropolis makes so many protected markets?

A country which finds itself in this stage of evolution and consequently presents the full gamut of the ills of overpopulation, is Germany. Inadequacy of agricultural products, extreme misery in the poorest section of their proletariat[21], intensive emigration,

---

[21] The following extract, reproduced by the *Journal* of 26 December 1910, of a study by Mr. E. Smith which appeared in the *Contemporary Review,* concerning food in Germany, shows what the poor do to feed themselves in this overpopulated country *par excellence*:
The Freibank of a German city is a most interesting place, though few tourists visit it, and those who do seldom know much about the commodities exposed there for sale. In Berlin there are four of such buildings, all situated in the poorer quarters of the town, but as a rule one Freibank suffices for each great industrial city; whilst in Hamburg there is net one at all as yet, owing possibly to the fact that that town is so close to the ports where we send our worn-out horses that this peculiar institution is not so necessary there as elsewhere.
For the Freibank is a meat market of a very strange sort—not a meat market specially for either cattle, horse or dog, but a meat market for the poor, and for the poor alone, and so safeguarded by laws and regulations, and watched by

police and inspectors, that it would be very difficult as well as disgraceful for any well-to-do people to buy their meat supplies there.

And the reason why there are all these rules and penalties connected with this particular German meat market is because the meat sold there is all under the ban of the veterinary inspection, which has been conducted in the *Schlachthaus* and *Sanitas-Anstalt*, and is flesh taken from animals that are so much diseased that either the flesh is lowered in value by the disease or else is actually infected by disease. But in the latter case the disease germs have always been completely killed by prolonged scientific sterilisation.

The flesh of animals who have become feverish from more than twenty-four hours suffering from accidents is also sent to the *Freibank* for sale, but if the animals have been slaughtered before that length of time, it lies in the discretion of the inspectors whether the flesh should be sent to the Freibank or into general sale.

The *Freibank* is to all appearances an open meat market. You will see little to shock you in walking through it. The people who are shopping here are poorer looking than is usual, but that is all the difference that you would notice from any ordinary market. The price of the meat, too, is lower, but not so low as one might suspect from the sort of stuff sold. It must be at least one-fourth lower in price than the same sort of meat would sell for outside.

Neither would the tuberculous cooked meat stalls offer any shock to the ordinary sight-seer; that the meat there is almost black in hue owing to prolonged and high sterilisation would not surprise the sight-seer, for the press of poor people round these stalls is so great that it is difficult to get near enough to see the meat at all, unless, like myself, one goes prepared for the spectacle, and so is willing to wait with the crowd and push for a place in advance of the others. It is not by taking a Cook's ticket to tour in Germany that one gets to see the way the Germans live. Neither is it by living in hotels and taking a saunter into the cathedrals and palaces German sanitarians are as skilful as our own, and their standard for healthy meat is as high as ours. That does not mean that the animals from which the meat is taken must be absolutely free from disease—neither in England nor in Germany could such a standard be kept up — but it means that whatever disease has affected the animal the flesh has not been infected. If the fish or muscle has been infected by disease then in England the, carcase is condemned *in toto*——both flesh and fat.

In Germany they do things differently. There they have three standards for their flesh fit for human food :—

(a) The same standard as our own for general use in the city.

(b) The *Minderwertig*, or lowered in value.

(c) The *Bedingt Tauglich*, or conditionally fit, i.e., flesh which would be unfit for human food unless scientifically sterilised.

That the highest standard is not unduly severe can be shown from the official reports, where we read of very doubtful flesh (as we should think) which nevertheless was able to .pass as high class. For instance, we read the following from the Report from Berlin of 1908: —

> Special account of tuberculous animals in which the defects — irrespective of the diseased parts — were limited to certain quarters of the animals' flesh.

And annexed to this description we read of how these animals have been divided into the four different standards: some parts stamped as highest standard for use in the city; some parts sent to the *Freibank* as *Minderwertig*; others sent as *Bedingt Tauglich* to undergo scientific sterilisation; whilst other parts were altogether condemned as unfit for human food.

Any of our medical officers of health would have a very different way of treating this business.

Again, we read in the Report of the same year from Munich (page 7) of an epidemic of foot and mouth disease which had twice manifested itself in the neighbourhood in the spring and autumn of that year, and it is recorded that they have it all. Quite happily, the rate of births has begun to drop, slower than in France, but surely nevertheless.

While waiting for de-overpopulation, Germany, whose massive surplus population threatens to destroy the famous "European balance" is locked in mute struggle with England, since the latter has an immense colonial empire and therefore hinders German expansion, — while England, which preceded the German empire in overpopulation and consequently in colonialism and extreme industrialization, regards this rival with contempt, who steals its commercial flows which are less easily protected, given that it has abundant and therefore cheap manpower. Germany also feels imperiled by its neighbor Russia, whose overpopulation is rapidly accentuated, and which is irritated by the commercial competition which the Germans have brought to its own soil by force. Finally, it is jealous of France, whose overpopulation is less intense than its own, which doesn't justify, as far as it's concerned, the

---

a number of cattle and swine which had been affected with the complaint were slaughtered, and after the diseased parts had been cut away, and the flesh steeped in boiling water, this flesh was sent into the general circulation of the city shops as sound and healthy meat.

French Proletarians, if your heart tells you... *repopulate:* you will also have your *butchers for the poor.*

But your poverty will make The Fatherland more prosperous!

possession of a more important collection of colonies than its own.

As for France, what remedy do its patriots, whether the self-seeking capitalists or the "sucker" proletarian ones, offer against the menace of Germanic overpopulation? — As for the rise of the French overpopulation, the former pretend not to see it and the latter don't realize that if war must one day be the result of the pressure of the German population, this cure, which is worse than the disease, will only hasten the birth of a conflict and its bloody solution.

*
**

But the capitalists exploit the colonies in more ways than commercially. In indigenous production, they also find material to be stolen, whether as a pure and simple appropriation of the earth and its products, with an organization of labor which is worse than the supposedly abolished slavery, or in the form of taxation, — exorbitant taxation which leads to famine, as in the unhappy English Indies, where, ever since the conquest, the Hindu peasants eat three times less than before while furnishing a large part of the cotton and cereals that England needs.

And there, we might find, had it not already been demonstrated elsewhere, the proof of the lack of subsistence, that is, of overpopulation, in the colonizing nation. This proof would be found in the nature of the imports from the colonies: these are,

145

almost exclusively, agricultural products, food commodities. Doubtless they also bring primary materials for non-food manufacturing industries: metals, wood, ivory, rubber, etc., but what they go in search of mostly is wheat, rye, buckwheat, corn, rice, manioc, coffee, sugarcane, oils, fruits, and even livestock. And what is exported in exchange: manufactured objects which the indigenous population doesn't need, but the need for which has to be stimulated in them.

But here my heckler will respond that subsistence is not lacking, since it is found in these colonies. I start by asking him not to confuse the effect with the cause: colonialism is the effect for which overpopulation or lack of subsistence is the cause. I would tell him, then, if he has the idea, as unusual as it is for his mentality, of extending the question to the whole Earth, ignoring its division into warring States, that I've never claimed that the Earth was overpopulated relative to its highest power of production and that it cannot feed more inhabitants than the present number. What I do say is that it's overpopulated relative to the existing products in every epoch in a country, that it has been this way to some extent, and that it will always be this way as long as they refuse to use the necessary means to balance the two factors of population: birth and subsistence.

How do they go about obtaining this lacking food, whose existence they find outside the country where they live? By constant colonial war, and at the price of war between civilized countries which often results. Wouldn't it be wiser to limit the population to the available subsistence?

*
**

War is *business*...

What a good cause of enthusiasm of patriotically prolific imbeciles, — but does this amusing "phenomenon" actually exist: proletarians who deliberately give their wives children in order to make more soldiers for "his" country! ...

No, obviously, that can't be real. It would be beyond grotesque. The reasons why proletarians tend to have so many children comes down to ignorance and carelessness, except in the case of a few contemptible brutes who knowingly make a lucrative career from their reproduction. We're not in ancient Rome, where, due to the appeal of rewards which, without doubt, our procreatomanicacs would love to bring back, paired brutes intentionally produced cannon fodder. Isn't it Rome, also, where we got the idea of "proletarians" from, i.e., citizens who can only be useful to the state through their families, — proto-cannon fodder?

Wars were frequent there. The rulers had such a need for soldiers that they created the institution of "alimenta children", i.e., male children maintained by

147

the emperors (Trajan fed up to 5,000) and by certain cities and destined, upon reaching adulthood, to fill the gaps made by the wars in the armies.

It's probable that, despite the ignoble character of the thing, the Romans found it quite legitimate: the patriotic religion was there to darken their minds and help them find this murderous force-feeding entirely natural, just as today it is accepted by most of the proletarians, who are brutalized by the same means, whom the capitalists can lead to the international slaughter when they feel the need.

But the foresight of our bourgeois is far ahead of that of the Roman rulers: they don't feed the fodder to the cannon by force; they were content to get it born and later they take them all, sending to the profitable massacre everyone who survives the trial of poverty caused by the overpopulation which they have willed, created, and maintained.

For, it's paving the way for murderous overpopulation when you keep silent about its effects, keep silent about the means of avoiding it, and track these more highly evolved Neo-Malthusians, when they provide their saving propaganda. We should expect neither light nor tolerance from the bourgeois on this point: their class-interest forbids them from doing so. On this matter, as on everything, the emancipation of the workers will be their own doing. The elite of the proletariat has begun to realize this, as we saw at the beginning of this study, but the great majority of the proletarians remain ignorant of the natural law which governs the populating of the Earth and on which, consequently, their existence depends.

*
**

According to this law, formulated by Malthus in 1798 in his *Essay on the Principle of Population*, if nothing hinders it, the population will grow indefinitely in geometrical progression (1,2, 4, 8, 16, 32, 64, 128, 256), while subsistence only grows arithmetically (1, 2, 3, 4, 5, 6, 7, 8, 9).

This dual formula of progression is above all a mathematical image, intended to show the eternal mismatch between the multiplication of men and that of subsistence. However, if the arithmetical progression isn't perfectly right, since it depends in part on human industry, the geometrical progression is absolutely true.

Since Malthus's day, science has brought mankind ways of temporarily growing their means of subsistence faster; however, after the pressures of progress in the agronomic science have passed, normal progression and even stagnation returns, when it isn't in fact regression, by virtue of the law of diminishing productivity to which cultivated land is subject.

But the principle of the biological law of population is far from being contradicted by these facts. Malthus's law remains true, in the sense that the population has a constant tendency to grow beyond its means of subsistence.

If a given population, in a limited territory, has no foresight in its procreation (and, collectively speaking, this is what happens always and everywhere), the phenomenon of overpopulation occurs, i.e., an imbalance arises between the population and subsistence. For it's not the population that controls subsistence, subsistence always determines the population. Only Zola was able to show us the opposite in action... in a novel called *Fécondité*!

All the phenomena of population are therefore relative to subsistence, — the available subsistence, that is, since men can eat neither ideals nor hypotheses.

It hardly matters that the capitalist system, by many organic flaws which, added to so many others, condemn it by, at various times and places, bringing obstacles to a temporarily faster and wider multiplication of subsistence (for example, by keeping cultivators ignorant, depriving them of machines or chemical fertilizers, and reserving some arable land for luxury items); it hardly matters that, through waste, it keeps a part of the population from participating in the existing subsistence; it hardly matters if the capitalists have more than necessary: defective production and bad redistribution, products of society, in no way weaken the law of population, which is a natural fact.

Let me be clear: this is far from a justification of the misdeeds of any capitalists. The destruction of *their* society is a goal we must never lose sight of, an urgent task. But, both reason and experience prove that, if capitalist society were ever done away with; the law of population would continue to act with mathematical rigor; on this point no society, whether collectivist, communist, or constituted by some other mode of egalitarian association, could ever live without taking this into account. When, in society, a state of overpopulation occurs, there will be malaise, and if humanity were only a single people, there would still be wars — social war and, ultimately, a reestablishment of the original order of things. Of course, that's for the future and we must stick to the present, which is our only concern. It's with the same concern for the actual and real that I am reasoning about the only *available* food.

This represents the vital potential. But when there is a surplus of population with respect to the totality of possible life, then life, failing to be brought back to society, in *quantity*, to the desired level of subsistence, is brought back there in *quality* in each individual who, by the fact of overpopulation, is deprived of some of what is necessary, when he is spared complete elimination by death.

Then, for the proletarians, the facts of poor redistribution are added to those of overpopulation. And we say: Who, in this case, is deprived of what is necessary? Not the capitalist, since he has his share — and, by and large, everyone else's. It's only the proletarians, who must look to their master, the lazy bourgeois, and the owner of the instruments of production and their products, for the meager wages which the latter is happy to trade for his labor, — a wage which overpopulation, through the competition of the unemployed, reduces to the lowest possible level.

Thus, the unavoidable equilibrium is established, to the detriment of the quality of life, for the proletarians alone, painfully, by famine, poverty, prostitution, and disease.

What, for example, is tuberculosis, which the doctors who spread something other than the official truths, call *the poor man's disease*, if not the state of physiological degeneration brought on by deprivation and overwork, which are due to a lack of adequate food, — to overpopulation?

Hasn't Niceforo experimentally proven that the repeated deprivation of the vital necessities of both ancestors and descendants in a certain part of humanity, this monstrosity has been constituted: a *poor race*?

Established among the proletariat by the poor quality of life, the equilibrium is also introduced there by the brevity of existence.

The following statistics[22], drawn up by Doctor Jacques Bertillon, not suspected as coming from this distinguished repopulator, are considerable. (And yet they meant little to their author, who continues to be a ferocious anti-Malthusian).

For every 1,000 people born on the same date, the following numbers remain alive:

	per 1,000 rich	**per 1,000 poor**
After 5 years.........	943	665
” 10 ”	938	586
” 20 ”	866	486
” 30 ”	796	408
” 40 ”	695	396
” 50 ”	557	283
” 60 ”	398	172
” 70 ”	235	65
” 80 ”	37	9

---

[22] According to *Croitre ou disparaître*, by G. Deherme.

*
**

And it's in the name of The Fatherland, this idol whose feet are bathed in mud and blood, this "spook" as Stirner calls it, this "cloud", to use the epithet which the nationalists apply to abstractions which correspond to nothing real, but which they forget to apply to the one they exploit, — it's in the name of The Fatherland that the proletarians have just been asked, not only to maintain their poverty, but to aggravate it even more!

As we've seen, they have no interest in acting like patriots, any more than in having many children. Instead, they have every advantage in displaying their lack of patriotism and infertility. The only argument of the bourgeoisie, i.e., preparation for war, should therefore leave them indifferent, — or, even better: hostile. Let them think: the less dense a country's population is, and the less patriotic it is, the better a chance it has of escaping the evils of war.

War, from the start, is ignoble. That's enough to condemn it. But it might be unavoidable; it isn't that way by essence, but only through human stupidity.

Next, it's made for the profit of the capitalist bourgeoisie. What do the proletarians get from it then, they, in sum, who furnish the cannon fodder? Military servitude, the burdens of armed peace and those of war, disability, and death.

It's true that some, among the survivors and those who are unfit for combat (the latter are often ferocious patriots), find the satisfaction in the wish contained in this odious and often-formulated popular notion, when everyone is suffering an extreme case of overpopulation: "There are too many, we need a *good* war to make room!" It's up to the proletarians to decide whether they prefer to improve their conditions through organized murder — in which, naturally, they themselves might end up as the victims — or if, morality to one side, it might be smarter to bring some caution into their sexual activity and keep a "good" war from becoming necessary so that everyone can have a place in the banquet of life.

For this desire is determined exclusively by the overloading of the labor market, where the working class is most keenly aware of the fact of overpopulation. And so, through careless procreation, the proletarians create overpopulation, and this overpopulation heightens competition, leading some of them to this monstrous clamoring for a war which will ease conditions for the survivors, — a demand which will quickly be sanctioned, for, in this case, natural and social determinism will create a war.

War will come because there must be colonies to accommodate the superfluous population of the overpopulated nation, and to place the surplus product of the national industry at the same time as procuring the subsistence lacking in the metropolis. It will come because the necessary financial means must be extracted through the exploitation of the weak countries so that this poorer part of the stronger nation can enjoy the illusion of pecuniary assistance from the government. It will come because, when the proletariat, driven to death like a beast of burden, is about to rise up, — quite fruitlessly, in this case, for overpopulation has also created, inside its own class, the enemies of its liberation: "yellows", policemen, taskmasters, professional soldiers, etc., who would drown its rebellion in blood, — war is in the air, as they say, and the leaders, after having, as is only right, whipped the patriotism of the masses up to a fever pitch, wage it to keep the State, or their party which has the monopoly thereof, from disappearing: then, the shepherds lead the flock to the slaughterhouse...

For the capitalists, this, too, is good business: they purchase security, at the higher wages which inevitably follow the massacre, for a long span of years, in the same way that, by means of finance, they might purchase primary materials or advertisements. And they know full well that, thanks to the prolific breeding of the brutes, they will soon find their human livestock in abundance, for, as a distinguished murderer said a century ago, "a single night in Paris will make up for all that."

As for the ruins, if the venture doesn't work out, it's also the proletariat who will pick up the pieces. Is it not, definitively, forced to pay, in every situation, for the broken pots? Why is that? Only because it's the *proletariat*, that is, the *class of child-makers*.

On the day when he ceases to multiply inconsiderately, the proletarian, becoming stronger and more deserving of liberty, will soon be able to stand before the bourgeois class and tell it, even individually, in explicit or implicit terms, it hardly matters which: "Now I'm stronger than you. I'm no longer a proletarian in the ancient sense of the term: I no longer want to be one in the modernized sense either. I refuse to endure you parasites. Property is theft: I refuse to let you steal from me any longer. The day of reckoning has come. There is no longer any private capital. Capital is common to all workers and work is the only remunerative value. If you wish to live, then work."

*
**

In sum, whether, as per the socialists, the causes of war are found only in the evolution of capitalism, or, as the Neo-Malthusians, along with Darwin, more rightly find it in overpopulation, the proletarians have an interest in refusing to give their masters the cannon fodder they demand.

As the better proletarians have recently said, "Insurrection, not war!" The limitation on birth is a practical and permanent form of this insurrection, where individual efforts effectively and manifestly contribute to collective action, which additionally satisfies both the immediate needs and the idealistic tendencies of both the individual and the collectivity, — that is: the proletarians and the global working class.

May the proletarians, their awareness rising more and more every day, give a listening ear to the word, already scientific, but still timid, which travels across three centuries, from good old Malthus; may they listen to his disciples, the Neo-Malthusians, whose voice is more robust because they know more than their ancestor, and since, irreligiously, they can promote the tools of voluntary sterility which terrified his own religiosity; and they will learn the power they have to keep from turning out as cannon-fodder.

www.ingramcontent.com/pod-product-compliance
Lightning Source LLC
Chambersburg PA
CBHW031122250726
48655CB00004B/1804